1984

12

Michael A. Faletti
410 Grover Street
Joliet, Illinois

A
Pictorial
History
of
Burlesque

BOOKS BY BERNARD SOBEL

Broadway Heartbreak *(memoirs)*
Burleycue
The Theatre Handbook
The Indiscreet Girl *(a novel)*
A Pictorial History of Burlesque

A
Pictorial
History
of
Burlesque

BERNARD SOBEL

BONANZA BOOKS • NEW YORK

For Dr. and Mrs. Morris Dinnerstein

©1956 by Bernard Sobel

*This edition is published by Bonanza Books,
a division of Crown Publishers, Inc.,
by arrangement with G. P. Putnam's Sons.*

(B)

Library of Congress Catalog
Card Number: 56-10246

Manufactured in the United States of America

Table of Contents

Acknowledgments

The following friends helped in the preparation of this book: Virginia Carrick; John Gassner, Sterling Professor of Playwriting, Yale University; Thomas J. Phillips, Executive Director of the Burlesque Artists Association; Richard Williams, Managing Editor of *Theatre Arts;* Abel Green, Editor of *Variety;* Clark Kinnaird; Gorham Munson; Dan Healy; Florence Vandam; Harry Davies; Harland Dixon; George Freedley, Curator, and the staff of the Theatre Collection, New York Public Library — Elizabeth P. Barrett, William H. Mathews and Paul Myers — and May Davenport Seymour, Curator of the Theatre Collection, Museum of the City of New York.

1

As It Was in the Beginning

The history of American burlesque begins with a Greek classic and ends with a leg show. For all practical purposes, however, it began in the 1860's when Lydia Thompson and her British Blondes, all of whom wore tights, delightfully shocked New York audiences.

When it reached its peak in the early years of this century, burlesque was a composite entertainment that took its components from the minstrel show, variety, extravaganza, comedy "bits," and extra added attractions such as boxing bouts and the hootchy-kootchy. It owed its demise to Prohibition, the cinema, and the advent of short skirts when the sight of women's legs ceased to be a rarity.

But while it lasted, burlesque fulfilled several useful functions. It served as the poor man's clubhouse where, for an amount within the means of almost anyone, men could escape from nagging wives and business worries; it was also the ideal school for a vicarious sowing of wild oats and for learning the facts of life by way of glamour and merriment. It was also the proving ground for many of today's greatest stars of stage, screen, TV and night clubs.

Whatever vulgarity or indecency burlesque exploited, it represented "what comes naturally," a wondrous experience in sex, an experience to anticipate, realize, remember and enjoy again.

By contrast, this era, plagued by Freudian analysis and derivative gutter concentration on homosexuality, bisexuality, interchangeable hermaphrodites and other clinical complications, seems to have lost its *joie de vivre*.

The burlesquer of yesterday symbolized the typical actor who has only one

9

Aristophanes, classic Greek dramatist and poet, known as the "Father
of Burlesque"

Boccaccio, whose name is perpetually linked to stories told on the sly

object in life: to put on a perfect performance that will satisfy his audience. He was oblivious to conventions. He ignored social, racial and religious restrictions, sexual aberrations, class distinctions. He was a true democrat.

That old-fashioned term "rough diamond" fit snugly the personalities of the early stars of Broadway, both made and female. They had their conceptions of gallantry, they held the affections of their public. They were picturesque, what the French call "originals." They suffered, worked, enjoyed themselves, and had their eyes always on a possible chance of getting into a Broadway show. They were keenly aware of the American feeling for laughter.

The accredited father of burlesque was Aristophanes, fifth century B.C., playwright, poet, innovator and reformer, who chose parody as the racy instrument of his reforms. He spoofed current affairs; devised gags, puns, wisecracks. He brought the seduction theme into the theater. He played up fleshly descriptions. Twenty-five centuries later, American burlesque was employing the same devices in speech and action that were reduced to the lowest common denominator of popular taste.

The transition, however, was not as direct or simple as it seems. During the Middle Ages and on down into the eighteenth century, Italy made three contributions to the final form of American burlesque: the burletta, the Gesta Romanorum, and the *commedia dell' arte*.

Written in rhyme and entirely musical, the burletta, "a poor relation to the opera," may well have supplied the name of burlesque.

The Gesta Romanorum were anecdotes and pseudo-moral tales which served as source material for Boccaccio and, centuries later, with the addition of spicy anecdotes and topical off-color stories, furnished the pattern for the "bits" or brief comedy sketches which were the great laugh-getters of burlesque.

The *commedia dell' arte* played its part in the development of burlesque humor, for improvisation — ad libbing — was the test of the American comedian's ability and popularity. Certainly the influence of the Italian improvised comedy made itself widely felt, for the players appeared throughout Europe and penetrated to the British Isles, leaving their imprint on the English pantomime, the universal Punch and Judy show, and the immortal Harlequin and Pierrot.

But it was the English development of burlesque which affected the American stage most directly.

England saw its first burlesque, *The Most Lamentable Comedy and Most Cruel Death of Pyramus*, a take-off in *A Midsummer Night's Dream*, in 1600. In 1671, George Villiers set the pattern for future writers of "legitimate burlesque" in *The Rehearsal*, a spoof about Dryden and the heroic drama. Sheridan developed this pattern in *The Critic* (1779) which made sport of the sentimental drama and contemporary literary foibles; and Henry Fielding perfected it in *Tom Thumb, the Great* (1730) and *Tumble Down Dick*.

Meanwhile the entertainment had acquired two important fresh features: musical numbers and themes based on French parodies and revues.

Gay's *Beggar's Opera* (1728), by Henry Carey, was the first burlesque to have songs. It was followed two years later by J. P. Planché's English adaptations of French *féeries folies* (fairy-tale travesties) and revues (take-offs on current theater hits). "Fantastic affairs" intended solely for amusement, they stressed sex and were called extravaganzas.

The probable beginning of American burlesque was the importation in 1828 of the English production *Hamlet* by John Poole. First produced in London in 1811, this travesty originated what was to be called legitimate burlesque. The success of this work created a vogue for travesties on classical drama and historical themes — *Much Ado About a Merchant of Venice, Pocahontas, Columbus.* Soon managers began to import works of this type and native authors to write them. There followed a craze for take-offs on grand opera. *The Bohemian Girl* became *Bohea Man's Girl; Norma, Normer; Frieschutz, Fried Shots;* and *Hernani, Her Nanny.*

With these travesties there grew up a race of comedians and playwrights — William Mitchel, William E. Burton, Mark Smith, Charles Fisher, and John Brougham, the "American Aristophanes" — all famous, among other points, for their comic female impersonations. Their most popular successors were Carrie Sara and Alfred Nelson, and the Worrell Sisters — Sophie, Jennie and Irene — who produced the *Field of the Cloth of Gold* in 1868. This year marked the decline of legitimate burlesque. Interest had already begun to lag, thanks to the popularity of tights. It was to decline still more sharply with the advent, in 1869, of Lydia Thompson and her British Blondes.

The scandal of tights, which from the very first was the chief enticement of American burlesque, started on February 7, 1827, with the obscure Mlle. Hutin, at the Thalia Theatre, New York. It reached new heights on June 7, 1861, with Adah Isaacs Menken. This lady, well conscious of the beauty of her own figure, displayed herself in tights while strapped to a living horse in a play founded on Byron's poem, "Mazeppa."

The stunt fired the town with excitement, brought Miss Menken immediate fame, started her on a theatrical career which included triumphs in Paris, London and Vienna, and precipitated a flood of other Mazeppas whose one object was the exploitation of the female figure.

The reformers were horrified, but their perturbation increased when *The Black Crook* opened with an Amazon parade of legs. Oddly enough, this theatrical impropriety was quite accidental, due to the chance inclusion of a stranded foreign ballet troupe in a rather dull piece.

But the results were calculated. Commercial managers got busy and turned out plays like *The White Faun* and *Humpty Dumpty,* so that by May, 1869, Olive Logan was savagely denouncing the rage for nudity before the Women's Suffrage Convention.

"No decent woman," she asserted, "can now look to the stage as a career. Clothed in the dress of an honest woman, she is worth nothing to a manager.

Punchinello, whose drollery still lives in the Punch and Judy show

Harlequin humor in the *commedia dell' arte* seeped through to burlesque

Stripped as naked as she dare, and it seems there is little left when so much is done, she becomes a prize to her manager, who knows that crowds will rush to see her."

Denunciation of this sort, of course, swelled box office receipts and quickened the managers in the purchase of tights and the duplication of ideas. For the American burlesque, from its inception, overlapped other forms of light entertainment — travesty, musical comedy, extravaganza — causing, thereby, endless confusion concerning the status of actors and the nature of productions.

13

2

Lydia Thompson and Her British Blondes

The originator of the American burlesque show was a man named Michael Leavitt, but he admitted publicly his indebtedness to Lydia Thompson and her British Blondes, who opened up a whole new world of amusement when they took New York by storm in 1869.

Though her permanent fame rests on having popularized legs in the American theater, she referred to these anatomical members publicly as "limbs." Incongruity of this sort punctuated the life of this extraordinary woman. She was the accidental progenitress of American burlesque, but had no part in the debased form of entertainment modeled after her own. She aroused the reformers, but won the admiration of the most distinguished clergymen of her time. She sang songs which were so suggestive that they stimulated police attention, yet one writer described her as "the essence of refinement." Her "golden voice" made bad puns sound "poetic."

At the age of twenty in London she appeared in a shadow dance, a feature of *Peep o' Day*, a spectacular burlesque. For some time after, her progress was a matter of theatrical routine. Then, suddenly, she captured the attention of all London town.

The circumstances were colorful. In those days the English took the stage seriously — king, statesman, merchant and barrister found time to follow theatrical

Lydia Thompson as Robinson Crusoe, chaperoned by Friday

Caught off guard

Where's her summer reading?

activities and to attach significance to them. The press, alert to public or clique opinion, published supposition and prophecy, and flavored these with political or national propaganda.

Thus it was that the then-current appearance of Perea Nina served as an occasion for a prolonged journalistic discussion worthy of the perpetual question of disarmament. Perea was a dancer; a Spanish dancer; an expert. She was, in fact, so talented as to win simultaneously both public adulation and disapprobation. Even though people flocked to see her and acknowledged her supremacy, they feared that her virtuosity imperiled the status of the English dance muse. But just when it looked as if English feet, completely overwhelmed, would cease to twinkle and pirouette forever, Lydia came to the rescue.

She acquired, in some miraculous way, a knowledge of all the feats which the Spanish dancer performed, along with the secrets of her grace. Then the young Englishwoman engaged in a kind of dancing duel with her Spanish rival and matched and outmatched her every step, twirl, whirl and posture.

"Showing a true Englishwoman's spirit, she vindicated the honor of her country while demonstrating perfection in a type of dancing heretofore deemed impossible for an English artiste to acquire." It was a great moment for England and a great moment, certainly, for Lydia. She became the toast of the town and the idol of the theatrical world.

She began to make American stage history when she became the first English actress to bring over an entire company of her own. She made a permanent niche for herself in the annals of the American theater as the apostle, though involuntarily, of American burlesque.

The engagement of Lydia Thompson and the British Blondes precipitated a theatrical tempest of criticism, gossip, business, imitation and amusement. Long before the *première*, advance publicity had excited the erratic curiosity of the

Lovely Pauline Markham, one of the stars of the British Blondes

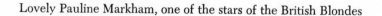

Casting reflections

Consciously coy and conscienceless

public, jogged up the reformers and aroused the suspicion of the hairdressers. Would the Blondes disrupt the nation, shatter the moral code and harry the last inhabitant to perdition?

In 1869, in honor of the occasion, Wood's Theatre was renovated and "reorganized" at an advertised cost of thirty thousand dollars. *Ixion, ex-King of Thessaly or The Man at the Wheel*, by F. C. Burand, was the opening attraction. It was a dull juvenile story about miscellaneous mortals and jumbled mythology.

The plot served as a framework for elaborate costumes, songs, dances, local allusions, sarcastic comment, imitations of swell dandies and German benders. Lydia Thompson made a beautiful and shapely Ixion. Harry Beckett played Minerva, wore black mitts, and carried a reticule. Pauline Markham was lovely as Venus. Ada Harland as Jupiter executed a number of marvelous twirls and twists and "could not have been more graceful, by Jove." Lisa Weber did a song number called "Walking Down Broadway" which became a town hit.

The entertainment may have been disappointing to those who expected outrage and rape, but the critics managed to be shocked. Some based their objections on the wavering standard of personal morality; others on the aesthetics of the theater.

"To represent Minerva with a fan and whiskey flask," remarked the New York *Clipper,* "Jupiter as a jig dancer, Venus with a taste for the cancan, is all done, we suppose, in a laudable spirit of burlesque, but we could almost hate Miss Thompson and her assistants for spoiling this pretty story."

Another critic complained: "It is impossible to give an idea of this sustained burlesque. It resembles an Irish stew as one minute they are dancing a cancan

Reclining, yet alert to any possibility

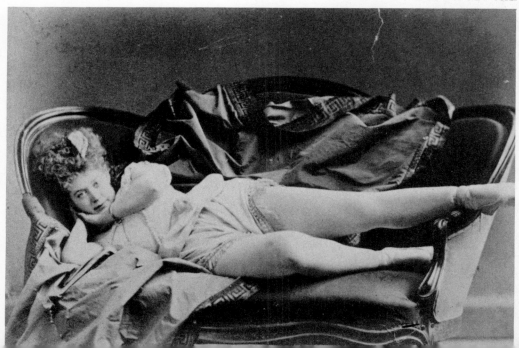

and the next singing a psalm tune. It is a bewilderment of limbs, belladonna and grease paint."

One writer summed up the Blonde situation by saying: "The propriety of visiting the Blondes is a question which each individual must decide for himself. The number of individuals who have decided this question, by the way, is something astonishing."

The male population, after the manner of males, favored it generally; while the females regarded it as a thriving menace to the home and fireside. Straightway the rebellion against legs directed toward *The Black Crook* veered to the Blondes.

By today's standards even of musical comedy, not to mention night clubs and what remains of burlesque itself, with its bumps and grinds, the ladies of the Thompson company made but sparse display of their figures. Those of the first and second rows, as well as the principals, wore over their covered legs a semblance of skirts, a foot in length, of thinnest mull with countless flounces.

To Lydia herself, however, such matters took on the importance of art in the abstract. She discussed tights as Einstein might have philosophized about the theory of relativity. She disclaimed the honor of having worn them first and stated once definitely that a Mme. Trevis, and not she, was the first to disport them. On one occasion she took pains to remark that it was not the wearing of tights which was indecorous, but the manner in which they were worn, and to illustrate her principle she cited Shakespeare.

The fame of the Blondes grew rapidly and, despite adverse comment, artists

Peripatetic?

Watchful waiting

Copious lines lent luster to this
British Blonde

"The Jersey Lily" Langtry, vaudeville and stage star whom Edward
VII adored and Queen Victoria
detested

THEATRE COLLECTION, NEW YORK PUBLIC LIBRARY

and authors joined the fast-growing army of admirers. The young Brander Matthews, who would later be mentioned as Professor in the Drama Department of
Columbia University, must have been among these, for he wooed and won one
of the original beauties, Ada Harland, who soon left the company and became
absorbed somehow and oddly enough in American university life. Another
British Blonde, Eliza Weathersby, was the first wife of Nat Goodwin, matinée
idol, who later married, among others, Maxine Elliott.

Soon the stage door of the theater, located in an alley, was the shady mecca
for admirers. Here they congregated in such great numbers that the police had
to mobolize and brandish their clubs.

Nor was the Blondes' fame confined to New York. Lydia played the country
to immense audiences and mixed notices. Everywhere the Blondes were a huge
success. While the reformers and the ministers ranted and railed, the customers
stood in line for seats. North, South, West, beauty triumphed everywhere.

In Chicago Lydia horsewhipped an unfriendly newspaper editor; in New Orleans, on learning that the actors of France were destitute, victims of the 1873
depression, she promptly put on a benefit that netted them five thousand dollars.
Years later, in 1899, the French public returned her generous act with a benefit
in which no less an actress than the Divine Sarah Bernhardt took part.

As a legitimate actress, Lydia had played with the best, from Richard Mansfield and E. H. Sothern, the younger, to Mrs. Patrick Campbell. Her final appearance was in 1899 at a testimonial benefit at which W. S. Gilbert read a spe-
cially written farewell, and where the performers included Cyril Maude, Edna
May, Beerbohm Tree and Lily Langtry.

22

Eliza Weathersby, first in a series
of Nat Goodwin's wives, which included Maxine Elliott

THEATRE COLLECTION, NEW YORK PUBLIC LIBRARY

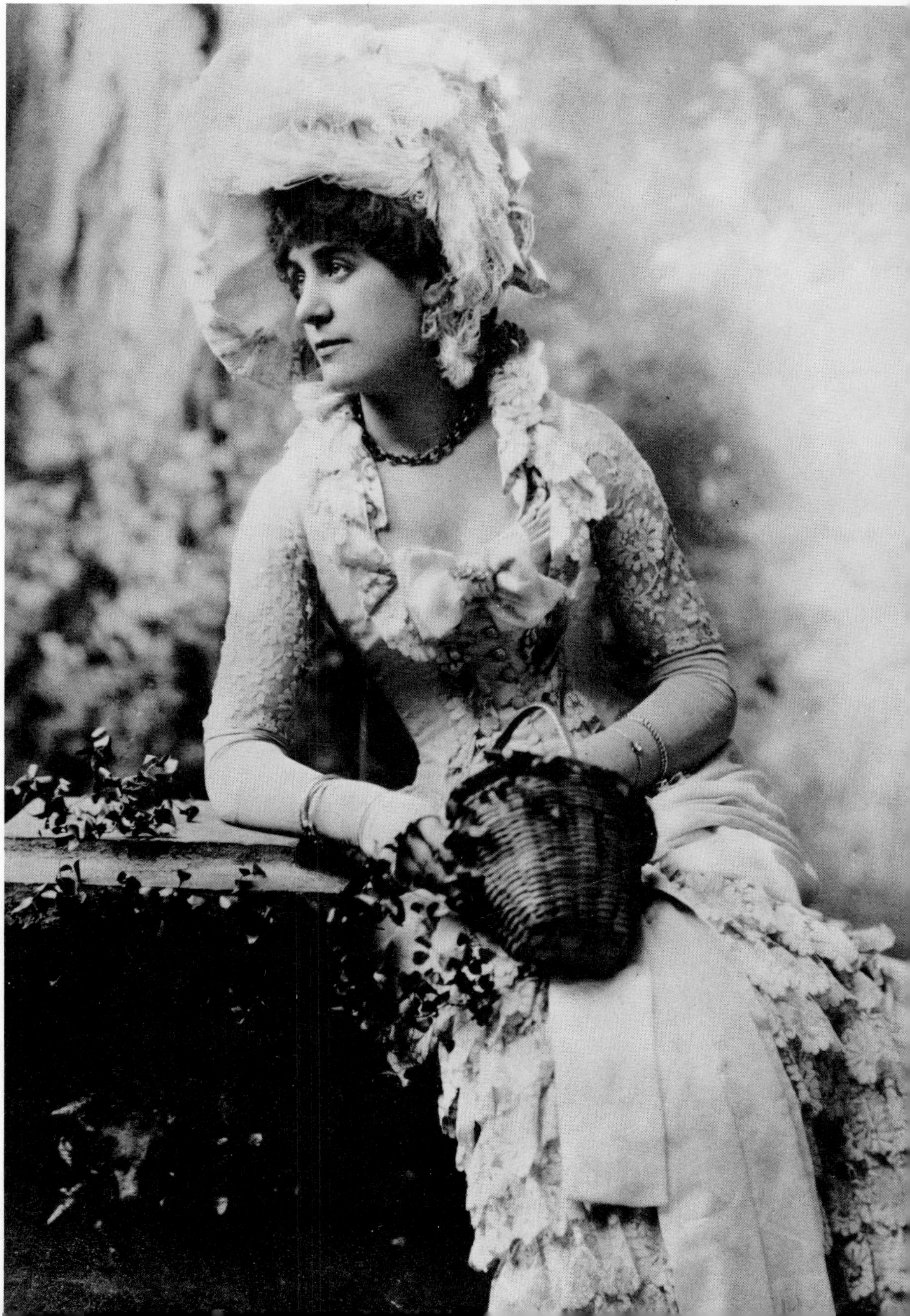

3

The Origins
of American Burlesque

Although Michael Leavitt, pioneer of American burlesque, credited Lydia Thompson with introducing to America the kind of entertainment which served as the model for his own, he admitted also that he had borrowed generously from contemporaneous forms of entertainment — minstrel show, variety and extravaganza.

Up until the nineties the minstrel show was an integral part of American recreational life. This all-male performance owed its beginnings to the old southern plantation where the slaves celebrated their leisure moments, their joys and their griefs by singing and dancing in a manner that was distinctly their own.

The creation of the first professional minstrel show (1830) is credited to Thomas D. Rice, who assembled plantation songs and dances around a central pattern and required his all-white performers to blacken their faces with burnt cork. He brought a new character to the American stage, the old southern Negro in ragged clothes whose walk had a peculiar shuffle. The minstrel show itself was built on a set pattern that the audience anticipated and enjoyed.

The orchestra was banked backstage. In front of the musicians upstage stood the black-faced troupe with the white-faced "middleman," or "interlocutor," who was the progenitor of the modern master of ceremonies. Seated in a semi-circle were six end men, performers who played the "bones," pieces of wood that approximated the sound of castanets, and the "tams" or tambourines.

24

Poster illustrating overlapping extravaganza and burlesque

At a given signal the interlocutor enunciated a phrase that became a cliché for decades: "Gentlemen, be-e-e seated!" And in response to this grandiloquent adjuration the minstrels sat down and the show began.

The first part consisted of songs and gag interludes between the interlocutor and the two end men. The second was called the "olio," derived probably from a Spanish word meaning mélange. It was a condensed variety show made up of quartet singing, terpsichorean novelties including clog, soft-shoe and pedestal dancing, and the inevitable female impersonator who was often starred. On one occasion, angry customers almost mobbed a company because they suspected that the female impersonator was actually a woman.

While the stage was being set for the third part, or afterpiece, the orchestra gave a brief concert which was followed by a song-and-dance finale called a "general ruckus" or "walk-around."

In their earliest days minstrels were known as "wagon shows." Then, as the size of the troupes increased and finances improved, they traveled by train in private cars. Affluent groups had show trains with titles like HI HENRY'S MIN-STRELS painted on the sides of the cars to impress gawking villagers at the railway station.

During the days when minstrelsy flourished, living was cheap, free from tax complications and inflation. Hotels made special concessions to theatrical folk. Somewhat typical, for instance, was a contract drawn up by a hostelry management and Duprez and Benedict's "gigantic" show, October 17, 1852, during its twenty-seventh tour. The terms specified that the rooms be clean, warm and light; that the guest would pay for bar bills and washing; and that he would sleep two in a bed, one bed in each room.

Obtaining food was a simple matter, for the minstrel could gobble up, with a five-cent glass of beer, enough free lunch to last until the next meal. But paying the rent was often so difficult that he avoided doing so by jumping out the window and making a nocturnal getaway, a practice which landlords halted by placing iron bars on this same window.

Eventually Rice brought his show to New York where it captivated the public and promptly inspired a series of imitators, among them the famous Christie's Minstrels, which began an engagement at the Mechanics' Social Hall in 1864. Several seasons later, Christie's successor, George Herring, continuing under the old name, took the troupe to London and scored a tremendous hit.

Eventually minstrel shows became so popular that they toured the entire country. In some odd instances, real Negroes blacked up to represent colored minstrels, realizing that the public wouldn't attend a show unless the performers wore burnt cork.

The minstrel show made an important contribution to American music. It was for Christie's Minstrels that the sluggish Stephen Foster was prodded into writing many of his melodies. Minstrelsy also preserved the jigs and songs of the carefree Negro. And the mournful, tattered minstrel with his banjo reflected

"The Divine Sarah" Bernhardt,
benefactress of Lydia Thompson

the Negro's patient resignation in the ballads adapted from spirituals and the mammy lullabies.

Among the famous minstrel shows were McIntyre and Heath, Primrose and West, Williams and Walker, Hi Henry, Lew Dockstader's and Haverly's.

Prominent among the minstrel stars were Chauncey Olcott, the famous Irish tenor, Eddie Leonard, the soft-shoe artist, Paul Dresser, brother of Theodore Dreiser and author of "On the Banks of the Wabash Far Away," and George "Honey Boy" Evans. Evans appeared under the management of Cohan and Harris with about a hundred performers in the finest minstrel show ever produced, a production which marked the climax and the passing of that form of entertainment except for current revivals in motion pictures and television.

Variety, another component of burlesque, came into existence with the Civil War. Originally a for-men-only show to be found in beer halls, it threw off its disreputable trappings with a change in name and developed gradually into a form of entertainment that glowed with talent and attracted mixed audiences.

The new name, vaudeville, had what might be called a snob appeal, for French terms, because of the very fact that they are not widely understood, are prone to impress the masses.

The term itself has a somewhat vague significance. It originated, according to one version, with Oliver Bassel or Olivier Basseliri, who sang and composed

Palace audiences loved "The Perfect Fool," Ed Wynn

Fay Templeton, variety and musical comedy star

songs and lived in a town called Val-de-Vire, corrupted during the time of Louis XVI to *vaux-de-vire,* and eventually changed to *vaux-de-ville.*

To Tony Pastor, more than to any other single person, vaudeville owed its birth in America. A New York beer hall proprietor in the seventies, Pastor had booked variety acts that were the ultimate in vulgarity when they were not actually obscene. Pastor shrewdly calculated that he could attract respectable people, both men and women, to his beer hall if he presented a bill of clean acts. He opened on October 24, 1881, with eight acts of comedy, acrobatics, song and dance, headed by Ella Wesner, a popular male impersonator. The novel form of variety proved an instant success and within two years Pastor had a host of imitators, beginning with B. F. Keith and his partners, Edward Franklin Albee

30

NICHOLSON

Uncle Miltie Berle, "Mr. Television"

Bill "Bojangles" Robinson and his
famous stepping-steps dance

and Frederick Francis Proctor, who took vaudeville out of the beer halls into large, well-equipped theaters, built especially for the purpose.

Vaudeville soon developed far beyond Pastor's goal of cleaning up the old-time variety acts. More sophisticated and responsive audiences were a challenge to actor and manager alike, and a brand-new form of novelty acts, comedy and drama emerged.

— From a bill of eight acts, each limited to twenty minutes, managers expanded their offerings to as many as fifteen, which included well-written sketches, the best in musical and spectacular numbers, and tastefully mounted animal and magic acts. It was vaudeville that developed the headliner system. Managers offered top billing and high salaries to such luminaries as Sarah Bernhardt,

31

Eddie Leonard, popular minstrel,
famous for his soft-shoe dance

Bert Williams in his famous rooster
costume

With a banjo on his knee, the sad-eyed minstrel sang songs of the sunny South

Emma Calvé, Mrs. Patrick Campbell, whose names pulled in the intelligent, so-phisticated theatergoers of the day.

But the backbone of vaudeville were the men and women who played two-a-day year in and year out — Charlie Case, whose muted monologues moved audiences to laughter and tears; the Howard brothers, Eugene and Willie; Joe Jackson, the bicycle tramp; the four Marx brothers, now represented by the super-comic TV star, Groucho; the sensationally successful Milton Berle, "Mr. Television" himself; and a host of others — Ed Wynn, Bill ("Bojangles") Robinson, Fay Templeton, Eddie Cantor, Nora Bayes — who served vaudeville faithfully and well before going on to musical comedy.

The typical vaudeville performance was a development of that section of the minstrel show which was called the olio. It included all sorts of novelty acts: singers, jugglers, dancers, contortionists and ventriloquists. It became eventual-

33

Phil Baker, Bad Boy from the Bronx, first M.C. for the $64 Question

Elsie Janis, vaudeville and musical star, sweetheart of the armed forces, doing an imitation of Will Rogers' rope act

ly an overdevelopment lasting for hours, yet neither performers nor audiences ever seemed to reach satiety.

The various numbers on the program were announced on a large sheet posted over the proscenium. Later, page boys carried signs listing the name and the number of the act. During the last days of superrefinement electric signs appeared on both sides of the stage, serving as silent announcers.

Vaudeville bills usually included "brother" and "sister" acts which were very popular fifty years ago. Sometimes the relationship was that of consanguinity and sometimes merely a matter of nomenclature. Famous in both variety and burlesque were the Watson Sisters, the Kaufman Brothers, the six Brown brothers and the Rogers Brothers, who became Broadway musical comedy stars and who

Pat Rooney, who produced the first vaudeville tabloid musical

put on a series of geographically titled hits, including *The Rogers Brothers in Paris*. The greatest authentic sister act was that of Camilla and Rosa Ponselle. Both became Metropolitan Opera stars.

In the early days of the motion picture, the show concluded with a film which was then so unpopular that at the first flicker the audience rose en masse and walked out.

Some of the most famous stars of musical comedy made their transition from burlesque and variety to Broadway by way of the Palace, which was called the Mecca for aspiring artists.

Here was the place for establishing records. Here was the spot where Eva

Smith and Dale, seventy-year-old comics still going strong

Lew Dockstader, beloved star of his own minstrel show

Tanguay knocked 'em cold, Lou Holtz had 'em rolling in the aisles, Phil Baker snared the wiseacres with his stooges, Georgie Jessel telephoned his mother, Frank Fay did a consecutive-engagement marathon, Elsie Janis did her imitation of Will Rogers' rope act, Pat Rooney and Marion Bent introduced the tabloid musical, complete with chorus, scenic effects and special costumes.

The annual patrician novelty was Ethel Barrymore in James Barrie's *The Twelve-Pound Look.*

Among other famous players to appear at the Palace was the beautiful Lily Langtry — toast of two continents whose name was intimately linked with Edward VII, then Prince of Wales. Young Alfred Lunt was Langtry's supporting actor.

A memorable feature of Palace performances was the Monday matinee. Here the shrewd agents picked out the new talent, and the producers selected acts for their forthcoming musicals. The high point of the afternoon came with the introduction of notables when the spotlight floated over the parquet and revealed such theatrical luminaries as Florenz Ziegfeld or Charles Dillingham.

37

The third chief ingredient of Leavitt's burlesque show was the extravaganza. The early prototype of this mongrel genre was *The Black Crook,* which opened at Niblo's Garden, September 12, 1866. In honor of the occasion the management had remodeled the stage, constructed trick scenery and placed trap doors at strategic areas on the new boards.

The show more than outdid itself in justifying the extensive preparations and the lavish expenditures of cash and energy. One scene surpassed another in what a contemporary critic described as the "first attempt to put on the stage the wild delirious joy of a sensuality fancy."

There were Amazon parades of ladies in tights. There were breath-taking vaultings of demons and good fairies. There were wondrous transformations, shadowy grottoes, stalactites depending from an arched roof. There were innumerable coryphees in enchanting *divertissements.*

All this grandeur happily submerged the central melodramatic plot, which

Stalacta and the Black Crook provide a melodramatic moment in the notorious extravaganza

A bouquet of *Black Crook* beauties. This notorious extravaganza started American ballet on the way to becoming one of the greatest exponents of this international art

Early version of the cancan

was so puerile that the critics dismissed it with contempt. The *divertissements*, however, according to more recent critics, revolutionized the ballet spectacle in America. But the glamour of *The Black Crook's* ballets must have been dimmed for the few brave ladies who attended the early performances, because they sat in the parquet heavily veiled.

But if *The Black Crook* were famous for nothing else, it would still be a milepost in the history of the American stage for introducing the cancan.

The dance itself had a classic origin, its principal intention being to agitate some part of the female anatomy for the edification of the audience. The characteristic movements included "circling of the legs" — lifting one leg and rotating only the lower part, thus forcing the *derrière to* wobble; the "pigeon wing" — bringing the bosom into play by leaping forward, kicking high and throwing the shoulders back; and "carrying on the arm" — holding one leg up against the

Modern version of the cancan, from the picture of that name

cheek while hopping lightly on the other leg. The grand finale was the splits, generally performed from a running start.

There have been various versions of the cancan but the *divertissement,* as now routined, is practically the national dance of France, as familiar as the "Marseillaise."

Paul Dervas, in his book on the Folies Bergere, credits the cancan with being the first dance to exploit nudity. It was hardly nudity as we know it, however, for the nakedness was confined to the sparse area between the high silk stockings and the frilly drawers.

The cancan is peculiarly associated with the lives of two famous painters: Finette, one of Whistler's mistresses, had the honor of introducing the number to English audiences; and Toulouse-Lautrec's cancan posters shocked all Paris and catapulted him into notoriety.

41

4

Michael Leavitt
and His Rentz-Santley Shows

The minstrel show, variety, extravaganza — Michael Leavitt borrowed from them all and created an entertainment with a new twist.

From the minstrel show he took the opening of his performance — the first part, which was made up of songs, choruses and gags. From variety he took the second part, an assorted array of talents and artists called olio. The third part, the afterpiece or burlesque, was a development of the minstrel show walk-around — a grand finale by the entire company.

These technical divisions as here outlined persisted in all burlesque shows until well into the first decade of this century. The girls were always off in the olio, but the other performers appeared in all three parts, the variety artists doubling in the afterpiece.

Leavitt called his first show *Mme. Rentz's Female Minstrels,* thus indicating its relation to an already popular form of entertainment with the added draw of a sex variation. The name "Rentz" was good selling, also, as it referred to a well-known Continental show called Rentz's Circus. Later, he changed the name of his company to the Rentz-Santley shows, in honor of one of his greatest burlesque beauties, Mabel Santley.

He retained likewise the mechanical arrangement of the minstrel first part, the performers being seated in a half circle with an end man at each extremity. The Rentz-Santley circle, though, was composed of women only. This was Leavitt's new idea — having women act as end men or feeders to the comedians. They carried the title of "principal boy" and became a burlesque convention. Following the English custom, these boy-girls wore tights while the girl-girls wore gowns slashed to show their legs. The effect of this innovation cannot be approximated in these days when nudity constitutes so often part of the hackneyed routine of musical comedy and revue. In 1869, however, the effect of even semirevealed tights was sensational.

"New York hadn't seen anything like it," Pauline Markham declared. "Every time my leg made its appearance outside of the cut skirt it was greeted with great guffaws from some of the men present."

Mr. Leavitt's industry brought rich rewards, rewards far greater than even he could have expected. The first Rentz-Santley show, made up of sure-fire ingredients, packed 'em in consistently that season and the next and the next, with the result that "Mike" Leavitt's duties became so numerous and involved that he had to get someone to help him. He looked around for a good Man Friday, and found a boy in his teens named George Lederer who was to become, not so many years later, a theatrical producer of international importance, his biggest hit being *Mme. Sherry*.

Mr. Leavitt put young Lederer to work on a travesty of *The Mikado*, which at the moment was the biggest hit in New York.

Thanks to the success of this piece, Leavitt soon discovered that there was an eager public for the Rentz-Santley type of entertainment; so, being a good showman, he brought a new one out each season, anticipating the recurrent editions of such institutions as the Ziegfeld Follies, the Music Box Revues and the Little Shows.

The Rentz-Santley shows in the main were substantial entertainments, with a great deal of rough-and-tumble business. Tights were plentiful but nudity was undreamed of. There were no hootch dancers, and aside from the occasional *double entendre*, little salaciousness. The dancing, though not as expert as it is today, was good. Nevertheless, the emphasis on this part of the performance

43

represents the beginning of a new era — light entertainment which culminated eventually in musical comedy and revue.

The architecture of the playhouses might well have been called functional. Most of them, unlike modern edifices, had galleries or loges with movable curtains to conceal improprieties. Some of the theaters were built in alleyways with partially concealed entrances where patrons could enter and depart without being seen. No decent woman would voluntarily pass by a burlesque house. If she were forced to, she lifted up her long skirts gingerly to avoid contamination.

Many of the burlesque houses had boxes and loges that could be quickly screened with draw curtains so that love affairs which were in progress during the performance were discreetly concealed. "Whore's Row" was the connotative term that was applied to the last row in the theater, the row reserved for unattended ladies looking for escorts.

Leavitt was proud of his productions and went in eventually for pretentious stage settings, elaborate costumes and effects. He was tireless in his search for new talent and succeeded in placing under his management some of the most accomplished performers of the day — stars of such contrasting abilities as Emma Carus, Rose Coghlan, Eliza Weathersby, Marie Sheridan, Marion Elmore, Hilda Thomas, Pauline Hall, Ann Sutherland, Louise Montague, Ada Richmond, Lulu Mortimer, Mabel Santley and May Howard, the last two of particular importance from the standpoint of America's burlesque history.

Mabel Santley, whose name formed part of the Rentz-Santley title, became a favorite whose amatory conquests gave rise to all sorts of legends. In one southern city it is said that two gentlemen occupied a stage box, both equally anxious to win the star's favor.

As the show progressed, one gentleman left the theater and returned with a bouquet. The other promptly sent an usher for an enormous basket of flowers. The next moment, the first gentleman vanished, only to return, five minutes later, with a crown of roses.

To put an end to the floral competition, the second gentleman tore a flashing solitaire from his finger, enclosed it in his boutonniere and tossed it across the footlights at Mabel Santley's feet.

Five minutes later, while the audience watched aghast, one gentleman dealt the other a stunning blow on the nose. Then both proceeded to jump over the boxes onto the stage where they continued pounding each other.

"What were those fools fighting about?" asked Miss Santley, after the minions of the law had induced the belligerents to depart.

"About you, miss. Each one swore that you looked at him and smiled."

"They were both right, only I was smiling because I was thinking that they were everlasting idiots. Send that ring right back to the man who sent it and tell him that Miss Santley has all the diamonds she wants just now, but when she feels like purchasing more, she'll let him hear from her, C.O.D."

44

One of the first women in the Rentz-Santley shows to obtain personal recognition was May Howard.

Born in Toronto, Ontario, where her father was a grocer, her real name was May Havill. At an early age she moved to Chicago, coming subsequently to New York for the purpose of going into the Leavitt burlesque show. She was a handsome young woman with a figure whose every line was destined to be known to millions of eyes over the footlights and through photographic reproduction.

During the seasons of 1886 and 1887 she signed as leading woman with a new burlesque troupe, Bob Manchester's Night Owls, with Manchester and John Jennings as the principal comedians, and a company which included Lizzie

Female minstrels *à la mode*

Mulvey, Belle Clifton, Louise Bliss, Jessie Boyd, Emma Jutau and George W. Brown.

One year later she was the star of the May Howard Company, organized by Thomas E. Miaco and her husband, Harry Morris, a fine comedian who later joined the Weber and Fields organizations. *The Roman Fete* opened the first part of this show and the burlesque was *A Black Sheep.*

Somewhat later, while playing an engagement at the old Standard Theatre, in St. Louis, Miss Howard's company established a record for gross receipts which remained unbroken until the showing of the Nelson-Britt fight pictures.

The May Howard Company became a leading attraction for a number of seasons, and though it suspended for a time, it came back again in 1897, with Miss Howard heading the company.

By this time the title "burlesque queen" was synonymous with the name of this shapely star. She managed her own company, "a leg show pure and simple," and endeavored to establish a standard of beauty by declaring that she would not engage any girl who weighed less than one hundred and fifty pounds.

At one time she delighted her admirers by wearing embroidered tights; and at another time she caused them the greatest consternation by declaring that she would never again appear in tights of any sort.

She graduated to the legitimate theater via a talent for comedy which she manifested first at the Casino under the management of Canary and Lederer; then in Donnelly and Gerard's farce comedy *Natural Gas;* and later in *Tillie's Nightmare,* starring Marie Dressler. About this time also she played a picture engagement in *The Vultures of Society.*

By 1921 she had retired in comfort to Chicago, but adversity forced her back into burlesque. Her return was ill-starred. While she was playing in The Great Galaxy Company, the Chicago Athletic Club made a ruling that all burlesquers were to be debarred from club quarters. Later she appeared in a suit against the management of *The Girls of All Nations* for discharge and arbitrary reduction of her salary.

Her most celebrated brush with the law, however, put her in the position of champion of the rights of actors. She sued Lew Watson, brother of "Billy" Watson and manager of the Washington Society Club, for opening her mail before it got into her hands, and had a federal warrant served on him by a United States marshal. In an era when mail and telegrams were delivered or forwarded at the whim of the management, with some suspicion that management was not always averse to steaming open an interesting-looking envelope, May Howard's action had important and lasting significance for the whole theatrical profession.

John E. Henshaw, who began his career as a boy with the Leavitt productions and fought his way up from burlesque to Broadway, where he was starred in *Baroness Fiddlesticks* at the Casino with Anna Fitziu, had vivid memories of the old Rentz-Santley days. "The show itself," he reminisced, "was free from the features that were characteristic of burlesque. The words 'damn' and 'hell' were

May Howard, first lady burlesque star to be dubbed "Queen"

never used on the stage — a terrific offense. If you uttered either word, you were called over to Mr. Leavitt's office the moment you left the stage and reprimanded. There were no *double entendres.* Tights, of course, were the sensational feature of the show. The girls all wore them, but they were masked with bloomers and short skirts which covered almost half the thigh.

"In San Francisco, we had advertised that we were going to put on the can-can. Mabel Santley did this number and when the music came to the dum-de-dum, she raised her foot just about twelve inches; whereupon the entire audience hollored 'Whoooo'! It set them crazy. Yes. Just that little gesture — the slight suggestion. The outrageousness of it spread rapidly. It became the talk of the town. The theater was jammed, as a result, for three full weeks.

"It's amusing now to recall, and perhaps incredible, but seeing a woman's ankle in those days was a novelty. Men would stand on the street corner, and wait and watch for girls to cross the street so they could see them raise their skirts. A rainy day would be a rich harvest. Not always, though, could we present the cancan. In some towns the police would be our nightly companions, watching the show like hawks to see that no naughty steps were exhibited.

"Though I have been on the stage all these years, I have never seen a better behaved troupe than this Rentz-Santley Company. In comparison with present-day companies they were saints and saintesses. Leavitt was a strict disciplinarian and he would not tolerate any foolishness. He was something of a general, very severe, but very likable. No theatrical organization today has the regulations we had. Printed on our contracts was a list of rules by which we had to abide. We were commanded to conduct ourselves as ladies and gentlemen at all times; advised that we were traveling with an organization that commanded respect in every shape and manner; and cautioned against committing a misdemeanor that would reflect on the show. And many a person was fired simply for breaking the rules."

Having demonstrated his abilities in the United States, Leavitt began a pretentious international campaign: took a complete Rentz-Santley show to England; brought foreign companies here; enjoyed many European tours; got the habit of crossing the Atlantic regularly, in something of the grand manner of the impresario.

The variety of his interests seemed only to stimulate his imagination when he put the American production of *Adamless Eden* into rehearsal. He engaged a staff made up entirely of women — women doorkeepers, ushers, managers and press agents; after which he organized a female orchestra of twenty to provide the music.

The Rentz-Santley series of shows lasted about ten years, during which period they deteriorated, underwent changes in management and finally succumbed to competition. By this time, however, burlesque had become a native theatrical institution, The pattern, as devised by Leavitt, persisted until 1890 and still persists, in parts, in the routine burlesque shows of today — a pattern made up of minstrel show, variety, and remnants of the English type of burlesque on opera, drama, and extravaganza.

Among the first shows to spring up after the Rentz-Santley productions during the years 1870 to 1880 were the Ada Richmond Burlesquers, Ada Kennedy's African Blonde Minstrels, the Victoria Loftus Troupe of British Blondes, H. C. Miner's burlesque of *Pinafore*. Ida Siddons, star of the Mastodon Minstrels, was famous for her rope jumping and fire dance. In 1879 Mary Fiske's English Blondes introduced *Dutch Justice*, a famous afterpiece which showed a court scene with Irish and German comedians, prisoners, and lawyers squirting siphons at each other, and a judge trying to establish order with a club or sledge hammer.

Louise Montague, a British Blonde principal

The history of some of the companies is noteworthy for the length of their runs and the fidelity of the public to the same old thing: the joy of recognition, welcoming back the same stars, laughing again at the familiar wheezes, stage business, bywords and *double entendre*.

Some of the prominent burlesque players of this period were B. C. Hart, Ethiopian entertainer, famous for his "Old Black Joe"; Gus Williams; Louise Montague, "the ten-thousand-dollar beauty"; Lillian Hall; Mlle. Zittella; Bobby Newcomb and Rosa Lee who, before playing in burlesque, appeared in *The Necromancer* in 1873, before Duke Alexis, uncle of the Czar of Russia, here at the time to hunt buffalo with General George Custer.

5

The Complete Show

Making due allowance for minor variations on the theme, the format of a burlesque show has remained much the same throughout its checkered history . . . As soon as the doors of the theater open, everyone rushes in, crowding, shoving, cussing, laughing and adding his personal share of uproar to the general hurly-burly.

The ushers, alert to any emergency, quickly show patrons to their seats, and a policeman or two keep their eyes open for anything that might happen.

Suddenly the tumult gives way to a respectful silence when the candy butcher — whose wares also include music, pornographic literature and pictures — walks up the aisle and takes his place at the center of the theater in front of the orchestra railing. His spiel is designed to get everyone in the proper mood.

"Your attention for just a few moments will be highly appreciated. As you folks are all aware, it is the usual thing, before the rise of a curtain of a burlesque show, to offer for sale some kind of a book in keeping with the type of show being presented.

"The show this week is *Moulin Rouge Night*. We submit therefore, for your approval, a French book which you will really enjoy. We have been offering magazines previously which have been causing quite a sensation, but what we are about to sell tonight will make all those other sensational books look like a lot of church sermons.

"On the inside of this book you'll find about forty-two of the spiciest, forty-two of the raciest, forty-two of the peppiest, forty-two of the sexiest stories that ever appeared in print.

"The stories are all translated into the English language and in the translation from one language to another they have lost none of their glamour or their pep. In fact, I defy anyone in the audience to read one page of any story in this book and then put it down without finishing it. Why? Because it leaves nothing to the imagination, because it calls a spade a spade, in plain black and white, using the same words that you use yourself whether they're in the dictionary or not.

"I haven't got enough time, alas, to go into all the details about all the tales in the book, but I'll try to give you a rough idea by mentioning two of them.

"The first story is called 'The Madame and the Sailor.' This story tells about a sailor in the French navy whose sweetheart ran one of those places in Paris where young men go for pleasure and ladies accept tips for their services. And — if you think a French girl doesn't know how to give service, you're crazy.

"This story tells you how this sailor went away on a nine-month cruise; how he was forced to stay on the boat and, of course, during all that time he never saw a woman. It tells you how he raced upstairs to Madame's apartment, very eager, and very excited; how he knocked on the door; how the maid answered him; how he walked into Madame's boudoir, a bedroom as we call it; how he saw the Madame there, just as she returned from the bathroom from taking a bath; how —

"Well, folks, you can put yourself in that man's place. Remember, he hadn't seen a woman for nine months and he was just rarin' to go. If the rest of the story doesn't make your hair stand right up on end, you're either getting old or there's something wrong with you. You ought to go to a doctor.

"The other story I want to call to your attention is called 'The Farmer's Daughter and a Traveling Salesman.' Of course we've all heard this story thirty years ago; how the clerk asked to sleep with the baby. Well, this is not that story.

"This is a strictly up-to-date version instead. It tells how instead of the salesman going to the farm, the farmer's daughter went to the city, met the salesman in a hotel, and what happened is guaranteed to give you a real thrill and also the biggest laugh that you ever had in your life.

"Now there are ten other stories, every one's as good and spicy as the two which I have mentioned. But that is not all. In the center of this book you are going to find a collection of the classiest art photographs you have ever seen in your life, photographs of young French beauties posing the way you'd like to see 'em pose; that is, entirely in the nude and revealing some of the most intimate parts of the female anatomy.

"Right now, also, I want to draw your attention to page seventy-four. I know that you'll positively be interested because you're going to find a photograph of a young lady lying down on a settee, or a couch as we call it.

"This young lady has no clothes on and you'll notice that she seems to have a very tired expression on her face as if she'd been doing a lot of hard work, and what kind of work she had been doing you'll have to use your imagination about.

"But if you have no imagination, turn the book upside down in this manner and place the palm of your hand over the lower part of this young lady's anatomy. What you'll see is going to surprise you. In other words you're going to see the sight of a lifetime. And what you see is nobody's business but your own. I thank you one and all for your kind attention."

Immediately the lights flash and the orchestra leader comes in with his musicians. A tumult of applause greets his entrance and from that moment on he becomes an intermittent performer in the show; for, in addition to directing the orchestra, he foils with the comedians and shouts wisecracks across the stage to the girls. He also manages to give the impression that he has had or could have any one of them, thereby exciting the envy of a large part of the audience.

At a second flashing of the light, the conductor taps his baton and the curtain rises, displaying the girls themselves. Simultaneously, everyone goes into a paroxysm of catcalls, hooting, jeers, applause, wolf whistles and glowing admiration.

At first glance the ladies appear to be visions of beauty. More critical observation, however, reveals heavy coatings of lipstick and rouge, copious applications of hair dye, and somewhat shaggy facial assets.

The Opening Chorus goes something like this: "College girls, college girls, we are the College Girls."

Then the oversized prima donna appears with a letter in her hand and reads: "I just received this letter from two millionaires, Mr. Clancy and Mr. Schwartz. Shall we show the gentlemen a good time?"

"You bet!" shouts the entire company.

At this cue, the orchestra starts playing "The Wearing of the Green" and the Irishman Clancy appears, saying, "By golly, where's Schwartz?"

Immediately the Dutch comedian rushes in, shouting, "Is dis de place?"

"Yes, it is," shriek the chorus girls.

"If dere's no udder place dan dis, dis must be de place."

The next moment a beautiful girl passes by and Schwartz shouts, "Hello, lady woman."

"Shut up," yells the Irishman to Schwartz. "That's no way to talk to a lady. Watch the way I do it."

Turning to the girl, he says, "Hello, you big bum."

The girl slaps the Irishman in the face; whereupon, seeing his chance to make a favorable impression, Schwartz walks up to her, saying soothingly, "Won't you have a drink, lady?"

"I never drink anything but champagne."

Enter waiter, carrying a magnum. The girl takes a huge draught of the wine and gets drunk immediately.

Schwartz, noticing that she is stewed, laments, "By golly, I could have got her that way on beer."

The show continues with monologues, songs, dances and other "bits" or com-

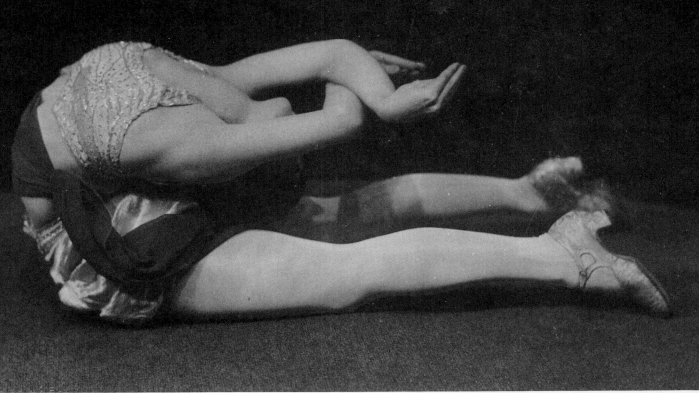

Sex takes a new form in this olio specialty

edy sketches, until the intermission, when half the house forms a processional and adjourns to the "can," the adjacent saloon, or to the sidewalk to talk over the dames or send a note backstage.

When everyone is back and comfortably installed in his seat, the candy butcher reappears, this time selling boxes of chocolates for a nickel, guaranteeing that one of the boxes contains for the lucky winner a solid gold ring with a diamond solitaire, pure and undefiled.

Part II, the olio, followed immediately. It was made up of sure-fire acts, or specialties, and included wrestlers, jugglers, contortionists, ventriloquists, equilibrists, artists who made music on water glasses, knife-throwers who hurled blades at living targets, acrobats, and singers of songs which are illustrated with colored magic-lantern slides.

From the standpoint of morality, the illustrated song in Part II served as a paradoxical interlude. It brought the ribaldry and the action to a dead stop with the introduction of a syrupy male singer and a series of magic-lantern slides, the same elemental slides that were eventually to supply the pattern for the modern motion picture.

The audience listened reverently while the vocalist sobbed out one of the many sentimental songs which were the popular musical fare of the day. The lyrics usually revealed how a beautiful, virtuous girl was undone by a preda-

53

Famous fighters who appeared in their own burleycue companies or served as "Extra Added Attractions."

tory villain, while the sickly sweet picture showed her dying, with her illegitimate child nestling in her helpless arms.

Oddly enough, although almost every man in the audience was concerned with actually, imaginatively, or vicariously getting one of the dames in the show into, bed with him, the story of the virtuous girl's downfall reduced most of the gentlemen to tears.

Part II also included "The Added Attraction," which was a burlesque development. It was the bait for attendance and specialized in hootch dancers. At one time or other, almost all the retired pugilists were added attractions, including Jim Jeffries, who wore two suits of long underwear in order to make his figure seem more shapely. Certain audiences were particularly partial to purring matches, an incredibly barbarous kind of bout in which the object was to kick the opponent in the shin until he cried for mercy.

Another famous added attraction was Sandow, the strong man, whom Florenz Ziegfeld managed and publicized in the beginning of his career.

"Mephitic" was the opprobrious word that a clergyman applied to the hootchy-kootchy, the most wicked dance in American terpsichorean annals. But sin being, as George Eliot declared, "a matter of geography," the hootch was wicked only by Occidental standards.

In the Orient the hootch or *danse de ventre* was a conventional *divertissement* made up largely of umbilical gyrations, since Orientals dance not so much with their feet as with their bellies.

The first lady to introduce the hootchy-kootchy to the American public was "Little Egypt," whose real name was supposed to be Fahreda Mahzar Spyropolos. A native, according to her own story, of Armenia, she came to the Chicago World's Fair to appear on "The Streets of Cairo," a feature of the Midway Plaisance in 1893.

Up till the day of her debut the World's Fair was a failure. The Fair, the first important one in the West, had cost millions. The innumerable buildings were handsome, the landscape gardening and educational exhibits noteworthy, the stimulus to trade exciting and apparently certain. But the Fair was no go. The public was not interested.

Just when the situation looked blackest, Little Egypt put in her appearance.

"Sandow the Strong Man," early exponent of male pulchritude in the raw

Little Egypt introduced the hootch, or belly dance, in 1893, when ladies and gents called that anatomical part the "stomach"

Crowds flocked to see her and incidentally patronized the Fair and the concessions. Simultaneously, clergy and press, outraged, described her goings-on, thereby increasing crowds and patronage. The World's Fair was suddenly a success!

Before a year had passed the show world gave birth to hundreds of Little Egypts, imitators who appeared in tent shows and museums for ten cents.

The dance was traditionally presented to the whining accompaniment of a wheezing instrument like a flageolet along with an insidious drumbeat. The authorship of the original hootch music, continuously disputed, has been credited to various countries.

In presenting hootch dancers at tent shows, carnivals and fairs, the barker would walk out on a platform and shout:

"Gather up closely, gentlemen, and get a surprise. See the free show!"

As the crowd assembled, the dancer would stroll out onto the platform. Her costume was always strictly Oriental: a short bolero with coin decorations, a white chemise, harem pantaloons and a wide sash. Her hair hung loose over her shoulders, an outward indication of abandon that was somewhat startling in the nineties.

Expectancy made the crowd tense, but while the perspiring barker made his oratorial spiel the lady would glance indifferently at the heavens or push aside her draperies casually in order to emphasize the intimacies of her costume.

"And now," the barker would cry, as he tapped his cane on the ticket box, "I take pleasure in introducing Little Egypt, the famous dancer who has turned this carnival into a conflagration.

"When she dances, every fiber and every tissue in her entire anatomy shakes

These wicked musical notes punctuated Little Egypt's gyrations

Nedja Ates helped wiggle the musical *Fanny* into a long run

like a jar of jelly from your grandmother's Thanksgiving dinner. Now, gentlemen, I don't say that she's that hot. But I do say that she is as hot as a red-hot stove on the fourth day of July in the hottest county in the state.

"Recently a prominent society woman, attired in men's clothing, came to see her, surreptitiously. The report was that she screamed for the police. That was a lie. The fact is that she screamed for the ice-man. Yes, this entertainment is hot stuff! Come in and enjoy the experience of a lifetime for ten cents."

When Metro-Goldwyn-Mayer produced *The Great Ziegfeld* several decades after the Chicago World's Fair, the picture showed Little Egypt doing her dance.

Almost as soon as this incident was flashed on the screen a woman of greatly advanced years started a lawsuit claiming that she was the original Little Egypt and that the film was injurious to her venerable reputation.

Eddie Foy, Jr., revives the phony knife-throwing olio feature in *The Pajama Game*

Whether or not this lady was actually Little Egypt was difficult to determine, for her name had become confused by this time with all the other Little Egypts and particularly with one who had made a sensation by popping out of a bird pie at a fabulous dinner party.

Establishing the historicity of the complainant involved a chase through research libraries and stage archives. A fascinating by-product of the research was the combination of interesting facts and near facts it revealed on the history of the dance itself.

The far-off origin of this sort of umbilical manipulation can be traced to primitive days when it had a tribal and religious significance as a dance of fertility.

The dance itself, however, was not Oriental in origin but Balkan, founded probably on an eighteenth century shepherd song. Almost a century later the principal motif recurred in two Russian dances by Lubomirsky and simultaneously in an anonymous German composition called "Bauchtanz" arranged by Allatara.

The first inclusion of the belly dance in a Broadway entertainment was in *Show Boat*, which gave an impression of the Chicago World's Fair with Little Egypt doing her dance. Since then revivals of the hootch have been seen in recent musicals like *Plain and Fancy, Fanny* and *Around the World*.

The prima donna Ljube Welitch astounded audiences at the Metropolitan Opera House when she began her version of Salome's "Dance of the Seven Veils" by walking down to the footlights and doing a belly dance.

Norman Bel Geddes, in *Arabesque* (1925), showed a group of Arab boys known as "hand" dancers doing a male hootch. Another male hootch dancer, who had a luxurious boat and the open sea painted on his belly, stopped the show cold at every performance of *South Pacific*. Recently, however, the all-time record for male umbilical gyrations was established by Elvis Presley, whose pelvic manipulations aroused, simultaneously, the disgust, admiration, condemnation and praise of millions of TV fans.

The show closed with an afterpiece that ran something like this:

The prima donna, surrounded by the entire company, says to the juvenile: "Now that you have inherited your rich uncle's money, what are you going to do?"

"I'll buy this café, darling, marry a rich widow and take a trip to Africa. And now, folks, if you'll join me, we'll all get aboard my uncle's yacht and start bounding over the billowy waves."

This subtle sequence paved the way for the grand finale, a patriotic display with the girls carrying flags of all nations before the backdrop on which was painted a huge star-spangled banner sparkling with electric lights. At a given signal the ladies maneuvered themselves into a straight line in front of the footlights, forming a blazing display of bosoms and legs known as the Amazon parade.

6

Sam T. Jack—A Foot in Each Camp

Until vaudeville became firmly established in its own respectable right, burlesque actors and vaudevillians were often interchangeable performers. Nowhere was this more strikingly illustrated than in Sam T. Jack's Chicago burlesque house.

Jack, who became an outstanding power in the burlesque world, started his career as manager of Mike Leavitt's Number Two Rentz-Santley company which went on tour. He took the nucleus of that company to Chicago and promptly started the theater which laid the foundation for his future success.

Sam T. Jack was an able man and a man of contrasts. Irreconcilable, often, was the divergency between his business methods and his personal principles. In establishing and operating the Sam T. Jack Theatre in Chicago, he put on shows that gave burlesque its early ill-repute; yet he used his own picture as a trade-mark to advertise the place. Though proud and ambitious, he did not consider it beneath his dignity to sit at the top of the steps in a hotel and wait for the girls in his show to return at night, checking off their names together with the hour from the list in his hand.

His Chicago burlesque house was situated at Madison and State streets, upstairs. The seating capacity was about six hundred, and downstairs there was a bar through which the girls had to pass. They got away with murder here. Jack's famous living pictures were often, as likely as not, merely exhibitions in the nude. Alexander Carr made an entrance adjusting his trousers. The police frequented backstage and front. This was the place that wives worried about when their husbands were out late; the place against which fathers warned their sons; the minister's symbol of iniquity.

All of which seemed to trouble Jack not at all. He went on making money, sending out companies, opening a New York house. An alert showman, he varied his policy from time to time to fit changing conditions with routine burlesque and adaptations of foreign plays.

His *Adamless Eden* company toured Texas and New Mexico, where the Mexicans regarded the girls as curiosities and followed them about calling them "gringos." Some of the Mexicans were so insistent in their attentions that a bodyguard had to be stationed about the adobe hotel where the girls had rooms.

When the company reached Tombstone, Arizona, they played the Bird Cage Theatre which adjoined a dance hall. The girls who were not appearing in the performance danced with the men and received half of the fifty cents charged for every dance. If the men opened champagne, the girls got a dollar on the bottle. On other drinks they received ten cents on the dollar. The regular salary was seventeen dollars and fifty cents per week.

Earning this salary was an exciting and even hazardous experience.

"No sooner," explained Annie Ashley, leading woman of *Adamless Eden,* "did we arrive in Tombstone than we found that a feud was going, in full swing, involving John Ringold against several brother outlaws.

"Every night the feudists would come to the theater. Sometimes they met there and shot it out, right in the theater. The boxes were built in a ring, like a horseshoe, and one gang would sit on one side and the other opposite. Once our black-face comedian, Billy Hart, was on the stage when a cowboy came in and shot the wig off his head, just for devilment.

"As soon as trouble started every one of us used to drop down and lie flat on her face. If we were dancing and the shooting commenced, the lights would go out and we'd lie down flat on our stomachs for protection."

By 1905, Sam T. Jack had developed a system of olio features never duplicated in Chicago: that is, a consistent tapping of the best-organized vaudeville of the period.

"A convenient alleyway made this nefarious arrangement possible," says Charles Washburn who wrote several librettos for burlesque. "It connected the Sam T. Jack Theatre with the Chicago Opera House on Washington Street. Up the alley the actors, headliners from the Chicago Opera House, often would rush with coats thrown over their costumes to appear under assumed names, five minutes later, on the stage of the Sam T. Jack show as features of the olio. The Chicago Opera House management may or may not have known what was happening, but the burlesque audience did certainly; packed the place to see Montgomery and Stone as 'Brown and Clark,' or some such name, in burlesque surroundings and at a burlesque admission fee."

Notwithstanding, it was the notorious Sam T. Jack Theatre which fostered the writings of William A. Phelan, a well-known Western journalist and one of the limited number of American writers who wrote regularly for burlesque. Many good quips and acts still in present-day musical comedy and revue are said to have been Phelan's originals.

62

Lotta Crabtree (1866), "Darling of the Mining Camps," where the admission price was gold dust

7

Honky-Tonk

Burlesque in the West started with what was known as honky-tonks, a term that was applied indiscriminately to dance halls, saloons and dime museums. "Wide open" was the policy of these nests of active crime, gambling, prostitution and fresh talent. Legitimate burlesquers disclaim relationship, but the stars were often the same, the entertainment similar, and the audiences usually identical.

The first honky-tonks started on the Barbary Coast, with John Considine owning a place called The Comique, in Seattle. Adjoining the theater was a dance hall. Here the male patrons — miners, Chinamen, Hindus and sailors — bought the girls drinks. And the girls saw to it that the drinks multiplied, for they got a check for every one rung up. Then as the show came to an end, and the place was about to close around five or six in the morning, the girls formed a line and collected the accumulated checks. And sometimes this line constituted a white slave mart, with a man standing on the side with a mallet in his hand and calling out: "Come on now. Pick one out. They're beautiful."

"Come on now. Pick one out. They're beautiful."

Often the girls were not girls but female impersonators. Incredible as this statement may seem, female impersonators dressed like soubrettes and chorus girls were decoys to attract patrons and induce them to buy drinks — an unexpected kickback to the Elizabethan theater where men played women's parts, and acting was akin to vagabondage.

Between the acts these impersonators would "work the boxes"; that is, visit with the male occupants, sit on their laps and help swell the receipts on liquor. Sometimes when the impersonator lingered too long in his enthusiasm to build up the check, discovery and a free-for-all fight ensued.

The business of real women working the boxes was much more involved and hazardous. Arrangements differed according to the amusement place. Usually there were two girl units — the one belonging to the show and the other to the house. In this case the girls attached to the amusement place would frequently be entertaining the men at the bar while the performance was going on. If

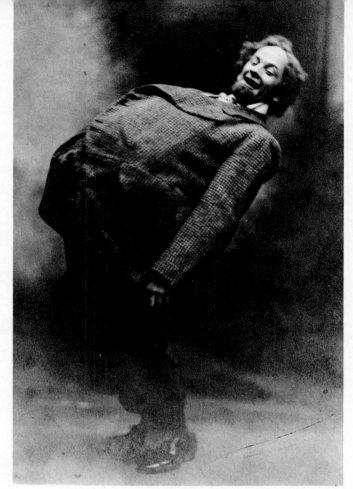

Leon Errol, whose fractious
knee had the audience rolling
in the aisles

an amusement place, however, was small and could not afford two sets of girls, the management required them to double on the stage and at the bar.

The complications were numerous. Frequently the husbands of the women were members of the cast and they would be singing or doing a comedy scene while looking on at their wives sitting on the laps of the amorous miners.

According to theory, women were never forced to work the boxes; and their efforts to evade this service were continuous and determined. Sometimes, when conditions permitted and their talents warranted, they were definitely released by contract.

But many a manager demanded that a performer's wife work the boxes, and if the husband objected, both he and his wife were fired.

Honky-tonk caught on and spread, first through the South and finally to the East, with ever more ingenious ideas for taking the customer. The Standard Theatre in Fort Worth, Texas, known also as The Silver Palace and owned by Frank Beque, boasted a restaurant, lunch counter, beer garden and two bars. Thirty-six girls were attached to the place. Their salary was fifteen dollars per week and a twenty-five-cent commission on each bottle of beer.

The boxes were hung with lace curtains and attached to the rear wall was a trough lined with copper. Into this, while their escorts were watching the show, the girls would empty their bottles of beer which ran swiftly back to the bar, there to be rebottled and resold.

The audience was picturesque: white-hatters, cattlemen, ranchers and cattle kings. Many of them wore revolvers in full view, often fifty-one calibers, an un-usually large gun, elaborate, beautifully etched, with carved bone handles. Bouncers were kept busy. Killings were frequent.

Out of this fearful arena of poverty, chicanery, gambling and prostitution came a list of stars that was noteworthy.

Among the most famous were Leon Errol, Grace La Rue, later a star of the famous Music Box Revue, Junie McCree, Frances White, Shaw and Lee, Jimmy "Schnozzola" Durante, stage, TV and screen star, huge-nosed mangler of the English language, and Harry Fox.

Fox and Jean Schwartz, a composer and another burlesquer, married the Dolly Sisters, Roszika and Jenny, musical comedy and revue stars. Both girls

Most imitated modern strut is head-shaking Jimmy Durante's exit

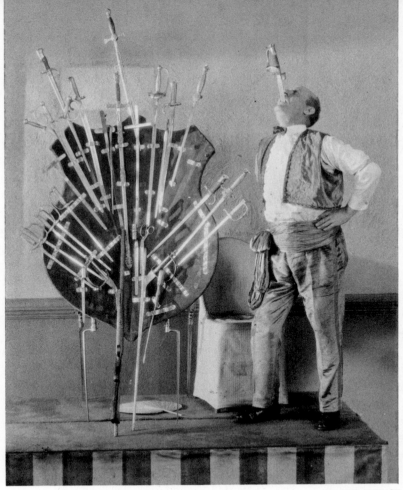

Knife swallowers added thrills to burlesque olios

shed their husbands, Fox and Schwartz, and went abroad where they became known as "the toasts of monarchs." In spite of their early declassé relationship with honky-tonks and burlesque performers, they became social arbiters on their own self-declared terms, for they announced, while playing in London, that they would never attend a party as entertainers even if the Prince of Wales were present. The titled Sassoon family rose to the challenge and invited the sisters to a party, not as entertainers but as guests. The results were surprising. During the evening Jenny was dancing with Prince Henry, and Roszika with the Prince of Wales.

The dime museums, another early form of native entertainment, ran twenty-four hours a day. First the audience would go upstairs and look over the curiosities, freaks and deformities: the fat woman, the albino girl, the living skeleton, the sword-swallower and the giant. Then everyone, after paying an additional twenty-five cents, would rush into the theater where the variety bill was on view.

67

The museum gave continuous performances. The actor worked on varying relays. Lew Fields states that he went to work at nine o'clock in the evening, worked till twelve and then went to bed. At five-thirty in the morning, he reported for the six o'clock show, after which he went to bed again.

The five A.M. audience was the most sympathetic and yet the strangest audience of the day, for it was composed largely of women of the tenderloin district. Their working day was over. Carefree for a few hours, they could enjoy the performance. And while they sat and cried over a topical ballad or applauded a bit, the few remaining men in the audience, sleeping by this time, were often snoring.

The dime museums were the training grounds for many important performers including McIntyre and Heath, Joe Weber, Lew Fields and Joe E. Brown, all of whom were forced to perfect their entertainment by innumerable repetitions of their acts. Joe E. Brown, at the age of nineteen, gave nineteen performances in a single day.

Honky-tonks and beer gardens eventually grew swanky and took on new names like rathskellers and cabarets. These high-sounding terms finally diminished into "night clubs." From these once-gay spots, three outstanding personalities were to emerge: Ted Lewis, immaculate with his "plug" hat, long-tail evening suit and dapper cane, scattering cheer with his well-known query, "Is everybody happy?"; "Texas" Guinan, Prohibition queen, famous for her greeting: "Hello, sucker," and for demanding applause for her performers with the

Joe E. Brown, dime museum alumnus, whose humor is as wide as his mouth

Ted Lewis, Chesterfieldian night-club master of ceremonies

words: "Give the little girl a hand"; and N.T.G. (Nils Granlund), the first important radio commentator. He sponsored nudity in The Silver Slipper and other night clubs where the word "ringside table" became a colloquial expression among the fussy and often gangster noctambulists.

Museums, saloon, dance halls, beer gardens — these made up the world of the honky-tonk. Back in the nineties they had achieved sufficient business importance to have their small circuits. And long after they disappeared, a few die-hards were still to be found spotted around the country. Not too many years ago, the last remnant of a museum chain stood in Chicago which bore the name Thurston's Folly Theatre. As late as 1929 the admission to Thurston's was ten cents. Hard refreshments, though, had given way to candy concessions and soft drinks, and the audience, having no chairs or tables, were forced to stand while a scanty bill of one or two acts was proffered for their dubious entertainment.

8

The School for Comics

In spite of its obscenity and immorality, burlesque had many good points. Prominent among these was a robust comedy which was cheerful and purging, a frank, normal acceptance of sex which puritanic America repudiated. As a result, American burlesque was the best school for the comedian. Here he learned to attract and hold the attention of a rowdy audience, an audience which, when bored, hissed, hooted and pitched eggs and tomatoes across the footlights. The training was savage, requiring youth, spirit and ability. It toughened the beginner, made him electrically sensitive to the capricious moods of the crowd.

In addition to the star comedians now called "top bananas," every show had three or four supporting comedians. They were stock characters and included, for the most part, the straight man, the Chink, the Dutchman, the Jew, the Dude and the Nigger.

The straight man who foiled with the comic was meticulously dressed and used high-falutin' language which contrasted sharply with his ill-dressed, illiterate partner. He was a "feeder," supplying the routine questions and answers necessary to putting over the jokes.

The "Chink" was attired often in immaculate white pajamas and wore a long pigtail, a forgotten symbol of the loyal Chinaman.

The Dutchman, a character made famous by comics like Jack Pearl, invariably used German dialect.

The Jewish comic, made up as a bearded, sloppy, stingy old man, was usually the ranking comedian of the company. Willie Howard was the first to break away from this stereotyped character.

The Dude was casually regarded as a sissy, but rarely with clinical homosexual implications.

The opprobrious term "nigger," so hateful to the colored man, never had an ugly connotation during the burlesque heyday. It did, however, limit the comic

70

Mendacious Baron Munschausen,
perpetuated by Jack Pearl

to menial roles such as bellhops, waiters, busboys and bootblacks. Nowadays, the word "nigger" and coon songs are taboo. Even the classic "Ol' Man River" must be edited.

Occasionally a new character was developed by a talented comic. Billy B. Van, who became a Broadway comedy star, added an extra personality to the comics when he originated an upstart Irish messenger boy called "Patsy Oliver," who wore a close red wig, short pants and gingham shirt.

Most of the comics were nationally known by their stock wheezes, catch phrases which provoked laughs — expressions that would seem tame today but were sure-fire in the nineties. Alexander Carr always remarked, "Toblitzky says"; Al Reeves, "Give me credit, boys"; and Sam Sidman, "Hot dawg." Bert Lahr was known by his gurgitating "Ga, ga, ga," Sam Howe by his "Oi, that's my horse," Dave Marion (Snuffy the Cabman) by his stuttering — a cliché that the younger Joey Faye revived.

Much of the humor of burlesque derived from optical effects. Laughter was evolved by the physical appearance of the comedians and the mechanical prop-

71

Bert Lahr in a typical burlesque "bit"

erties which they employed. They usually got a laugh the moment they made their entrance because of the ridiculous nature of their make-up and costumes.

Nearly all the comics wore ragged clothes, ill-fitting and grotesque. Certain ones wore enormous shoes, sometimes with enormous protruding papier-mâché toes. A favorite device was to use trousers too large for the body and let them drop down unexpectedly. Most of them wore an alcoholic red putty nose which made their normal proboscis twice the size, completely out of proportion with their normal features. Some wore flesh-colored skullcaps which created the impression of an extremely bald pate. Others wore "scare" wigs, so constructed that the false hair stood on end as if in a continuous state of fright. Certain comics, imitating strong men, padded their muscles and biceps and wore huge codpieces.

Stage properties which had a great part in the fun included the slapstick, bladders, bottles, rolled-up newspapers and phallic symbols. Two other important properties were the revolver and stage money. The revolver and the blank cartridge appear most importantly in the infidelity scene. Betting scenes were popular, with the dumb comic, always the dupe of the occasion, losing every cent he had. While the betting is in progress scores of bills are flashed, wallets displayed and dozens of pieces of worthless paper, colored with numerals and green ink, scattered over the bar and stage.

The "bits," however, were what made the comic. They furnished the bulk of the material on which most burlesque dialogue and action were based, and often these very same bits furnish the material for a large percentage of the sketches and black-outs used in present-day revues. Only a limited number of book shows dared to trust their fortunes to new dialogue and even these retained some bits intact, to insure stock laughs.

The bit, as so qualified, has probably never had a place in books on the technique of the drama. Nevertheless the bit must have a literary origin; must bear a relation to the Gesta Romanorum and the anecdotal racy stories which have passed on and on through the ages, cheered the life of the drummer, enriched the significance of the Pullman smoker, and perhaps supplied a plot nucleus for many a struggling playwright.

Considered technically, the bits have a basic pattern, a kind of formula. The typical bit always contains a menacing situation — a man caught with another man's wife, for instance. This situation, because of its universal applicability,

Bert Lahr, the gurgitating comic who has starred in revue and legitimate play

Dave Marion in his famous role of Snuffy the Cabman

is open to innumerable deviations. The second man can kill the first, all three can commit suicide, or turn the whole incident into a joke.

The humor of these situations is rarely evident in the printed script. For the laughs must be acted out and visualized. The personality of the players, the action and the phrasing created the laughs, and thus it was that burlesque companies could present perpetually the same old bits classifying these by a single term like the "lemon bit." Experienced burlesquers could describe an entire show by merely inspecting the properties. If there's a gavel backstage, then there's a courtroom bit; and so on indefinitely. They could play a whole bit by merely knowing the first line, "I'll see you around the corner," and the tag. The intervening dialogues they improvised.

74

The theatrical value of the bits never occurred to the burlesquer until around the 1900's when the Broadway shows began to use black-outs and skits, which were bits re-dressed with settings, costumes, effects, and much detail, assuming the importance of a substantial scene, three or four supplying most of the risible entertainment of the evening. Thus the burlesquers suddenly realized that they had been tossing away two or three times as much material in a single performance as was necessary to fill up two or three shows.

So fearful was the comic of the theft of his bits that he committed them to memory, never trusting them to paper. Yet the bits, as a matter of fact, were original only insofar as personal presentation was concerned. They were merely inheritances, often formulas from minstrel shows and medicine men, which were, in turn, the partial heirs of traveler, medieval troubador and perhaps a few crusaders.

But there was no need worrying about who wrote the bits, for there were more than enough to go around, and with repetition they always supplied an audience with the "joy of recognition." On the road, comics were popularly identified by their own bits just as they were identified by characteristic business or expression.

Thousands of burlesque enthusiasts will remember Leon Errol's now famous stagger; Jimmy Barton's drunk; Billy Watson's slide and his trick business with a burning cigar and ashes; Frank Finney's short arm; Bozo Snyder's silence and pantomimic business with a shoestring. They will remember also the *double entendre* connotations of certain phrases: Bill Campbell's "Sandy Beach, Pop-

Money-burning Joey Faye
in a burlesque bit

Straight out of burlesque is this discovery of a philanderer in a burlesque bit

per"; Sam Howe's "Oh, that's my horse"; Al Reeves' "Give me credit, boys"; Dave Marion's half mumbled "Well I'm a son of bitch"; Bert Lahr's "Oh boy! oh boy!"; Beef Trust Watson's tendency to pinch the posteriors of the nearest chorus girl. "Vas you dere, Sharlie?" identified the lovable comic Jack Pearl.

Though American burlesque was only a narrow section of world theater, its treatment of comedy afforded a retrospective glimpse of the theoretical and practical principles that governed writers for centuries. Until just recently, for instance, Aristotle was a dominating preceptor. He established the confines of the legitimate drama when he demanded that the dramatist restrict his story to the unities of time, place and action. Another arbiter, Carlo Gozzi, an Italian dramatist-theorist of the eighteenth century, declared that there were only thirty-six types of dramatic situation that could serve as the basis of a play.

Either because of rule or instinct, burlesquers concentrating on humor confined themselves to a few elemental emotions — lust, fear, appetite, greed and pain.

The following brief synopses of the "bits" illustrate the manner in which these emotions were used to stimulate laughter.

Cowardice

The straight man enters the scene with the comic. He carries a map which he says indicates a buried treasure. He leaves the comic alone, giving him a banana to eat. A ghost appears. The comic collapses when the ghost slips up behind him and eats the banana.

Predatory Man

A perennially popular bit is based on man's perpetual and often futile attempts to captivate woman. The straight man instructs the comic on how to win a woman by tempting her with some kind of magic charm, like a piece of jewelry or a love potion.

When a beautiful girl appears, the first comic tries the charm and is successful. The last comic tries the charm. He fails and instead of making a conquest he gets a slap in the face.

Insanity

One subject generally regarded as too harrowing for humor, though it was largely the basis of the great success, *Arsenic and Old Lace,* is insanity. Burlesque audiences have always found demented comics as amusing as that stock character of the drama and reality, the village idiot.

Malapropism

As language developed and people began to express themselves in oral and written speech, conversational comedy developed. Men and women alike were fascinated by the vagaries of languages. Bernard Shaw used this theme in *Pygmalion.* Weber and Fields and other comedians used it in burlesque in skits like "What's Watt Street" in which they became involved in linguistic complications.

One popular bit expressed the low-brow's contempt for the high-brow and took the form of a travesty on some higher form of art. In this skit the straight man delivers a pompous poetical recitation while the comedians, chorus girls and principals, acting in pantomime, make the various situations suggestive and absurd.

Liars

The liar's "bit" illustrates the public's contempt for politics. Two or three comedians boast of their ability to lie. "I can tell the biggest lie ever invented," says one, and he tells a whopper. The second comedian follows with another statement which is preposterous. Other comics also lie outrageously but the house comes down when the last one declares, "I know an honest politician."

Courtroom

Flugel Street had a courtroom scene in which the comic stuttered, the humor depending on the fact that the other characters were unable to understand the judge when he asked them how to get to Flugel Street.

Another variation of the courtroom bit, "Irish Justice," showed a seemingly important trial in progress. But when the accused and the witness take the stand, the judge, forgetful of all personal dignity, swats them over the head with bladders, hits them with a beanshooter and knocks them out with the official wooden gavel, the very instrument with which he has been endeavoring to keep the court in order.

The Bridal Night

The audience sees two adjoining rooms. In one, a bridal couple is packing a trunk by sitting on top of the lid. In the other, a farmer and his wife hear the bridal couple's conversation through the transom and misinterpret their behavior.

A variation of this bit shows the bashful young husband and the not-too-innocent young lady seeking lodgings for the night. From the moment that the curtain rises, all eyes center on the bed and all the stage business and dialogue is directed there also.

But, insofar as the young couple is concerned, the bed is absolutely useless. They never manage to get into it because of the explosion of a toy gun which breaks up the scene just before its consummation.

A. H. Woods built up a modern audience with bedroom farces like *Getting Gertie's Garter* and *Up in Mabel's Room* (1921).

Nuptials

Still another variation of this theme illustrates the varied manner in which the comics employed the same material.

The maid comes in and disrobes the bride. She takes off the bride's dress and reveals a petticoat and corset cover. These she removes, exposing the lady's underwear down to the chemise.

A moment later the old bridegroom enters. He wears his lounging robe and rubs his hands in anticipation. At that very moment the bride's step-ins fall away and she stands apparently nude, but actually in tights. The bridegroom kisses her and the lights go out.

Gazeeka Box

Some of the most popular bits employed extensive mechanical apparatus. The Gazeeka Box, for instance, was one of the favorites. As the story unfolds, the Top Banana tries to sell the Second Banana the Gazeeka Box, a flimsy structure which looks like a phone booth with a curtain.

When the Top Banana utters the magic word, a procession of beautiful girls exits from this booth. Delighted with the display of accessible femininity, the Second Banana buys the box instantly. But when he tries the magic word a monkey jumps out.

Crazy House

Some of the bit apparatus consists of simple house implements like the water sprinkler, used in the crazy-house scene. The sprinkler, however, causes plenty of trouble. The comic walks in, supposedly ill, with a doctor and a nurse in attendance. He wears what seems to be a regular nightgown but it is actually a kind of rubberized over-all robe that covers his body from head to toe.

No sooner does he jump into bed than the various attendants of the hospital begin to maltreat him. They fire guns, sound alarms, and make him so uncomfortable that he squirms out of the bed and jumps back into it time after time.

The lady, Gypsy Rose Lee, is on trial for a little matter of murder. Bobby Clark is the dignified presiding judge in a modernized bit from *Star and Garter*

Finally, a pert little nurse enters with a sprinkler, announcing that she is watering the flowers in her garden, and pours the contents of the sprinkler over the distracted comic until he is saturated from top to toe.

Dentist

A favorite bit displayed a dentist's chair bounded by handle bars, metal levers and a giant forceps. At the opening of the scene the patient enters solemnly, asks the pseudo physician for a treatment and timorously ascends the chair. Then the dentist gives the patient most unprofessional treatment, yanking him up, down and around him until he begs for mercy.

A variation of this bit shows a young lady going into a medical office for an examination. The doctor, one of the comics, begins a mock professional consultation. The pseudoscientific allusions to her anatomy invariably rock the house.

Dead Beat

Man's ancient weakness for gambling is the basis of the poker bit. An overconfident plunger meets a sharp operator and is soon robbed of his belongings. This sketch shows up the braggart who is detested by all classes in all ages and whose downfall makes the audience happy.

Human nature doesn't change. Rub the universal funny bone, a basic emotion, and a laugh is inevitable. And though there have been a thousand variations on the same old theme, the laughter runs on forever, pyramiding the cachinnations.

A new era in comedy was born about 1908 when Roger Imhoff discarded his whiskers and initiated a fresh type of monologue that was more difficult and that relied on cerebral dexterity rather than physical accouterments and props.

As Lew Fields once noted, early monologists always carried a satchel or a tray of pencils which gave them an excuse for opening their talk. When these were discarded, the comic was on his own. Attired in street clothes, his efforts to control an audience and make them laugh were multiplied.

The task of the comic was made difficult also by a campaign against dialect, initiated about 1940. For up to that time mispronounced words, broken English and foreign accents were sure laugh-getters.

But world war changed the American attitude toward the long-congealed opinion of foreigners. Frenchmen were no longer "frogs," Italians, "wops," nor Chinese, "Chinks." Burlesque discouraged its comedians from using Irish dialects, because of Sinn Fein activities. Germans ("Huns") lost all comedy value and killed off the old standby, the Dutch comedian.

After the shut-down of burlesque, the chances for the development of young comedians seemed hopeless. Then the Straw-hat or Borsht Circuit brought forth the incomparable Danny Kaye, Buddy Hackett and a few other fun-makers.

Recently, thanks to television, young comics and vaudevillians have a new chance to display their wares. The brightest newcomers take part in hours like Ed Sullivan's program; the very young and oddly assorted make their bows on Ted Mack's television show, today's version of Miner's Amateur Night.

9

The Wheels

After the Rentz-Santley Company's success had been followed by a quick rush of imitators, burlesque became an involved history of productions, personalities, litigation and social change. Gradually theatrical managers lost autocratic power, sharing it and sometimes yielding it to new entrants in the conflict — politicians grown from saloon proprietors to petty officials and big bosses who straightway cluttered up the already dubious history of burlesque with bribery, fraud, slugging and murder.

Scarcely did burlesque begin to develop as a distinct form of entertainment requiring theaters of its own than the politicians began to get busy acquiring them, trafficking in franchises, manipulating leases. Simultaneously they played the managers against the police who, under the misnomer of censorship, have long waged war against box office and public, with anything as the pretext.

In the late eighties and nineties there was little order to the burlesque business. Individual companies managed as best they could, "wildcatting" — arranging engagements here and there — fighting each other or forming friendly alliances. The first shows were routed around New York with what roughly corresponded to a booking office with Abe Leavitt, Mike's brother, in charge.

In the early nineties houses playing burlesque were Butler's Standard, St. Louis; The Howard, Boston; Smith's Opera House, Grand Rapids; The Adelphi, Buffalo; Theatre Comique, Washington; Central, Philadelphia; Westminster, Providence; Pence Opera House, Minneapolis; Alhambra, St. Louis; Olympic, Philadelphia; Park Theatre, Detroit; The Gaiety, Albany; Opera House, Newark; Gaiety, Troy; Monumental, Baltimore; Theatre Comique, Minneapolis; Buckingham, Louisville; Academy of Music, Pittsburgh, and the Lyceum, Washington.

In 1900, the management of the various companies and theaters, seeing the need for some sort of an agreement for the exchange of bookings and protection against contract jumpers, organized the Travelling Variety Managers' Association, with Samuel A. Scribner as president.

Naughtiest burlesque house in America, Howard's Athenaeum

At about the same time, the Eastern Circuit of House Managers was formed with George Krauss, president. The Empire Association was the name of the western circuit with J. L. Kernan and James J. Butler as the leading spirits.

Eastern and Western theaters together comprised a circuit which enabled one show to play 35 weeks. But rivalry between show owners and theater managers, always smoldering, broke into open warfare in 1904; and in 1905, the more powerful show owners withdrew and organized the Eastern — or Columbia — Wheel. This marked the beginning of the two circuits: the Columbia and the Empire (Western) Wheels.

Some of Columbia's first members were outstanding in the annals of American stage history, beginning with Sam A. Scribner, Columbia's first president, who fought the losing fight for clean burlesque. Harry Morris was an exceptionally fine comedian. A. H. Woodhull was one of the most effective and successful producers. William S. Campbell, comedian and manager, was the husband of Rose Sydell and it was he who rounded out the second longest run in history of burlesque — thirty years of Rose Sydell and her London Belles. William S. Drew managed the famous star in Cleveland.

Gus Hill, hard, sharp, but energetic to an astonishing degree, started life as an amateur athlete and at twenty-one was a wrestler and Indian club twirler — eventually the champion clubman of the world. Under this title he toured the

82

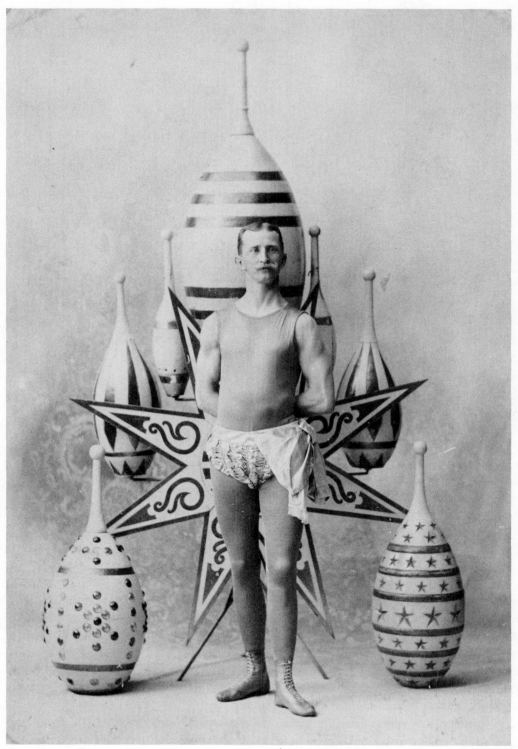

Gus Hill, hard-fisted burlesque producer, who ended up in a variety
act when he was in his seventies

Sam Bernard, a vaudeville and musical star who spoke a broad German dialect

variety houses, appearing with Maggie Cline, Montgomery and Stone, Weber and Fields, and Sam Bernard. This experience led him to theatrical producing, where his activities were highly varied. He produced *Through the Breakers*, the first play that Owen Davis ever wrote. He originated the comic strip musical comedies, *Mutt and Jeff* and *Bringing Up Father*. He had eighteen companies touring at one time: variety, musical comedy, burlesque and athletic shows.

The success of the Columbia circuit once assured, Scribner and his organization went in for rotarian improvement, picnics, slogans on clean shows, pompous statements of policy. Then Mutual Burlesque, carrying on the good work, put out a house organ with propaganda and solemn pronouncements of this sort:

Frank Taylor (St. Louis): That's a very nice little job you aspire to, but we do not require the services of an "inspector of girls' figures." We have no doubt you are quite qualified to perform such services, but we will continue to do all of the "inspecting" ourselves. You might obtain congenial employment in Brazil, where the "nuts" come from. This is merely a suggestion, however.

Frank Malley (Pittsburgh): Your jokes are clever, in a way, but they are not suited to Mutual shows. We are not conducting a Sunday school, but we strictly draw the line against that sort of humor. Try again. You undoubtedly can write, and we will be glad to hear from you if you will tone down your contributions.

This comedy sketch shows historic Herald Square, once the New York amusement center

The self-satisfaction of this house organ gave no hint of the decline of burlesque which was coming all too soon. Burlesquers organized their own clubhouses, had reunions, met daily on the sidewalk in front of Broadway's old Putnam Building, which was known familiarly as the "Beach," to chat about their act and their engagements. When the Putnam Building came down, the "Beach" was transferred to the Columbia Theatre; when the Columbia was demolished, the area in front of the Mayfair Theatre became the hang-out. But not for long. With the disappearance of the circuit the burlesquers wandered away on their own, to make their living as best they could. In the late twenties when Paramount Pictures sent out a call for burlesquers to support Helen Morgan in *Applause*, a picture about burlesque life, scores reported, glad even for a part as an extra at a small salary.

Historic Irving Square burlesque house

10

The Nineties

Though the nineties were gay, burlesque, curiously enough, lagged a bit. 1890 to 1900, according to *Variety,* was a period of slump. The theaters were run-down, and even though the entertainment was substantial and the comics good, the costumes and scenery were neglected.

In 1890, Reilly and Woods evidenced again the overlapping nature of burlesque and other light entertainment by transforming their variety organization into a burlesque simply through adding chorus girls to the afterpiece and interpolating numbers.

In 1896, Robey's *Knickerbockers* played Miner's Bowery six or seven times in one season with Burke Brothers, Edna Aug, LaRue Sisters, Edna and Grace, and Wise Mike, the Mule. Charlie Burke made a tremendous hit as an Irishman impersonating a Jew and singing "Rachel Goldstein," which was the talk of burlesque.

One of the shows that scored a hit, *The Twentieth Century Maids* (1902) owed its success to a burlesque of George du Maurier's *Trilby* called "Svengali," with Harry Morris sensationally successful in the title role, founded on Wilton Lackaye's contemporaneous portrayal in the legitimate play.

The most original show of the period, one which influenced greatly the character of later burlesques, was *The Bohemians,* September 7, 1896. The company included Harry C. Bryant, William B. Watson, Jeannette Dupree, and Billy B. Van. The production was so elaborate that it forced other producers to turn their attention to costumes and scenery.

The French Folly Company, an outstanding production, had a burlesque called "Adam and Eve's Daughter" and a first part called "Paris Life." The company included Sam Bernard, manager, Bobby Manchester, May Adams and Violet Griffen. The Watson Sisters, great favorites, were women of real ability, deservedly successful, who headed their own company.

About 1902, Weber and Fields took over the old Imperial Theatre and renamed it the Weber and Fields Music Hall, an act equivalent to a call to arms to producers of burlesque.

It was in 1899 that the name Watson grew familiar to the hearts of burlesque fans — first, through the organization of Watson's Beef Trust and then through the antics of "Sliding Billy" Watson. W. B. (Billy) Watson and his Beef Trust immortalized the pulchritude of the two-hundred-pound burlesque lassie, making her a popular type and a subject of marvel and tradition through the subsequent years during which woman has worried and tormented herself over diet and lines.

The arrival of Sliding Billy Watson on the scene and the resulting confusion so enraged Beef Trust Billy Watson that he issued a public statement, without specifying names:

The Watson Sisters, beloved burlesque heyday stars

THEATRE COLLECTION, NEW YORK PUBLIC LIBRARY

"Sliding" Billy Watson, no relation to Billy "Beef Trust" Watson

Billy "Beef Trust" Watson going strong

Billy Watson's "Beef Trust" ladies represented the ideal in female symmetry a half century ago

After being known as "Billy" Watson for the past forty-eight years, I have been amused at the absurdity of another claiming to be the original. Here and there over the country my friends called my attention to the claims of another performer who had the audacity to trade on the name that has gathered tens of thousands of friends in every State of the Union. . . . For sixteen years I have owned my own shows, and no one in all these years has addressed me other than "Billy," but I do sign checks as W. B. Watson. No one but a "nut" would do otherwise. The question may arise, "Who am I?" Well, I was born on the East Side in New York City. Went to the Allen School. Left when I was in the third grade. Was put to work as a furrier by my father. Worked up to twelve dollars a week. Saw some boys making more on the stage and left my position at twelve dollars to accept six dollars a week at the Globe Museum on the Bowery. Then went to the New York Museum at twelve dollars. Gradually, by working hard, I began to be noticed by leading vaudeville managers. . . . My first partner in a show was Harry Sefton, known as the "Dancing Spider." . . . After that I was associated with Harry Bryant for three seasons in two companies. Then I became the sole proprietor and have been my own "Boss" ever since. I AM THE ORIGINAL BILLY WATSON, AND SO SAYS THE PUBLIC.

The usurping Sliding Billy Watson, who entered burlesque in 1900, gained his name through his penchant for sliding across the stage to punctuate his comedy. He claimed to have slid into fame quite by accident when he was late for a cue and ran so fast onto the stage that he slipped and landed in a box, thereby breaking a man's stiff hat. It wowed the audience, including the man whose hat was ruined, and Billy forthwith worked the slide that was to make him famous into his routine. He denied that he put soap or anything else on his shoes, although he admitted to having a spring heel.

90

There were those who insisted, however, that Sliding Billy executed his slide with the aid of talcum powder and that furthermore the slide was actually originated by an actor named Charlie Burkhart.

With the production of Watson's Beef Trust, the history of burlesque and the legitimate theater came into juxtaposition in a peculiar manner. In 1931, Anne Nichols, creator of one of the most successful plays in theatrical history, *Abie's Irish Rose,* sued Universal Pictures for three million dollars, claiming that *The Cohens and the Kellys,* a picture, had been plagiarized from her work. The case was lost, however, on the ground that *Abie's Irish Rose* was founded on Watson's famous afterpiece, *Krausmeyer's Alley.*

Another outstanding personality to emerge in the nineties was the fabulous Rose Sydell.

In 1893, William Campbell organized the Rose Sydell Burlesque Company

SOME OF THE BEST BROILERS ON THE STAGE.

Say it with flowers — 1890

starring his wife Rose. She was one of the first American burlesquers to get her picture in *The Clipper,* an outstanding theatrical paper of the time.

She was the first burlesque queen to play to society when in Cleveland. She had her own show for twenty-six years.

It was she who popularized the song, "I Can't Resist You," after it was discarded by the publishers. It was she, also, who wore an ostrich plume so flowing and lavish that it reached from the brim of her hat to the hem of her skirts and trailed on the ground. And it was Rose Sydell, too, who managed to create the impression of having a diamond butterfly emerge from her breast by skillfully attaching it to her flesh with flesh-colored sticking plaster.

In the beginning, the company had difficulty recruiting chorus girls. Newspaper ads brought little response, for not too many girls wanted to go into burlesque. It was Rose who solved the problem by signing up good-looking wait-resses in the various hotels they stayed in on the road. In one season, she collected sixteen gorgeous chambermaids, waitresses and housemaids. It was the day of mutton-leg sleeves and high collars, a style that made almost any woman look voluptuous and well built. All the girls wore them when they were hired. But when the show opened in Cincinnati and the girls came out in tights for the Amazon parade, the audience hooted. The girls were beautiful but only three had decent figures. They were a sorry assortment of thin arms, bowed and bulging legs, scrawny necks and ugly thighs.

After that experience Rose conducted the tryouts in her own hotel room, requiring the aspirants to put on tights before signing up.

When the members of the company played Boston they got in trouble with the Watch and Ward Society. One of the girls in the company broke her shoulder strap and it fell off her arm. She caught it up swiftly and put it in place. Not quickly enough, though, for the Watch and Ward Society which had the entire company arrested.

Rose, however, was not incarcerated. The company was released and the judge lectured for forty-five minutes, finally forcing the Watch and Ward Society to apologize.

"After the trial," Rose recalls, "we went to Fall River. And if ever I felt like crying it was there. Everyone had heard of our hardships in Boston and in some friendly way had organized to gladden our hearts.

"At the end of the first act, as we came out to take our bows, the entire audience on the first floor rose en masse and cheered us, and every man and woman present had a black and yellow band across the chest bearing the word 'Welcome.'"

One of Rose's proudest boasts was that she shook hands with every president of the United States, from Cleveland to Calvin Coolidge. Instead of greeting Grover Cleveland with "How do you do?" she said, "I wish you health."

Cleveland didn't seem to notice her words until she passed by. Then he called her back and shook her hand twice, saying, "Thousands greet me here every day, but you are the first one to wish me health."

It was in the burlesque houses of the eighties and nineties that several present-day theatrical institutions originated — chorus girl contests, the country store, amateur nights and the expressions "Dumb Dora" and "Get the Hook." This last term was first used at Miner's Bowery Theatre.

Miner is an important and recurrent name in burlesque history as the Miners, owners of theaters, were among the first to shelter burlesque shows and sponsor burlesque entertainment.

Henry Clay Miner, head of the family, learned the show business as an advance agent for Signor Blitz, a magician, and as manager for *Buffalo Bill* at the Bowery Volks Garden. In partnership with Thomas Conway, he became later a theater lessee and builder, and in 1892, wealthy and influential, he was elected

An early burlesque queen at ease

to Congress. At one time he had extensive interests in traveling companies and had four theaters in New York.

The *Actor's Fair Bulletin* reports:

At Miner's Bowery Theatre in New York were given the first amateur nights in burlesque. Here the aspirants for footlight fame were given the opportunity to show their goods. The audience was at liberty to give full expression to their approval or dislike of the offerings of the contestants for the prizes. One Friday night, in October, 1903, at Miner's Bowery, a particularly bad amateur was inflicting upon a patient audience an impossible tenor solo. Despite howls, groans, catcalls, the artist persisted in staying on, when Tom Miner, who was running the show, chanced to see a large old-fashioned, crook-handled cane which had been used by one of the Negro impersonators. Quickly he had Charles Guthinger, the late stage manager, lash it to a long pole. With this, he stepped to the wings without getting into sight of the audience, deftly slipped the hook around the neck of the singer and yanked him off the stage before he knew what happened.

The next amateur who was giving an imitation of Booth announced that he would impersonate Richard Mansfield, when a small boy yelled, "Get the Hook!" The audience roared and the actor fled in dismay.

Many later stars including Fannie Brice, Joe Cook and George White endured the ordeal of the hook.

94

Ornate costume that made a burlesquer of the nineties observable

Roués and burlesquers made merry between rehearsals — not totally unlike the manners of today

Friday was amateur night at Miner's Bowery Theatre. It quickly became a fad and attracted hundreds of people who would otherwise never have entered a burlesque house. Eventually, amateur night was billed as a regular production, with spots saved for the feature performer. Among these was Jimmy Savo, who began his great theatrical career here. He juggled chairs, tables and wooden horses and won every prize in sight.

The country store, a popular feature of amateur night, consisted of a prize distribution of such edibles as apples, potatoes, flour and coffee.

"Get the Hook" and amateur nights survived to become a popular radio feature. It was on Major Bowes' Amateur Hour that Frank Sinatra got his first chance.

11

A Manager's Lot

"Virgin" was a provocative word that puzzled burlesque fans in the nineties, until it was displaced by the sophisticated current term "jail-bait," meaning "Lay off or land in the Tombs."

The companies were made up largely of girls in their teens who were runaways determined to escape paternal bondage, nymphomaniacs, servant girls hoping to improve their position, and stage-struck fillies with their eye on fame and fortune. Any appraisal of their behavior must be gauged by their general poverty.

Despite their disparity in status and purpose, engaging girls for burlesque was a difficult task. The ages-old prejudice against going on the stage in general was intensified when applied to burleycues. Often the managers would collect the required number of girls for a show only to learn at the last moment that their mothers, brothers or friends had dissuaded them from signing up.

Managerial methods differed according to individuals. Sometimes a hard-boiled showman was a softy at heart, but most of the time, through nature or necessity, he had to be severe. To strike an actor in the jaw was a part of the day's routine. Corralling the girls and keeping them in order and, what was more important, forcing them to keep their accounts straight were duties on which the manager's own job depended. In some of the companies, if a member of the company missed his train he would not only have to pay his own fare to the next town but sometimes a fine as well.

The strain of the complex duties of a burlesque manager was intensified where companies and audiences were constantly on the verge of outlawry. The manager had to have the strength of a giant, especially if he was the owner of a company with everything that he had in the world at the mercy of an emotional comic or an unexpected police raid. "Biff" Clark earned his nickname through the ease with which he'd knock down a man who dared question his authority.

Various managers had their particular methods for looking out for the welfare of the girls.

"I've made it a point in all my shows for thirty-five years," said Al Reeves, "to dismiss a girl who might corrupt the others, a girl who drank or did things out of the ordinary. It was best to remove her because one bad apple spoils the lot. I never use bad language in the presence of my girls."

Leavitt had rigid regulations concerning personal conduct; and his successor to the leadership of burlesque, Sam T. Jack, acted as a personal monitor for the girls of his company.

Somehow though, as burlesque flourished with its many companies and an influx of girls, there were, as in all ages and in all classes of society, personal deflections from codes.

W. C. Fields recalls that about 1895 it was a regular thing for the managers of the companies to get up and make a speech before a troupe went on tour, a speech which included this stern prohibition:

"We won't have any 'sketching' with this company. We won't stand for any 'doubling up.'"

Yet the show wouldn't be running two weeks before girls and boys would pair off, according to their liking. The liking, however, was sometimes oddly assorted, a stagehand with the prima donna and a veteran comic with a teen-age chorus girl.

A shrewd manager commercialized on these tie-ups. When he noticed that two people were living together, he cut their salary in half; and when the burlesquers complained, he'd say, "Two can live as cheap as one. You're doing that, ain't you?"

Sometimes, when business was bad, a manager exploited his own girl friend for the general good. Sometimes he effected an introduction to a local plutocrat who, in his enthusiastic admiration for the young woman and his general interest in the theatrical art, would supply sufficient funds to carry the company on to the next stop.

The average salary for chorus girls was fifteen or sixteen dollars until about 1901, when Harry Williams came onto the scene. His was a liberal management likened for decency and fairness unto that of the distinguished legitimate producer, Charles Frohman. He raised salaries from fifteen to eighteen, twenty and twenty-five dollars.

Other managers demanded a certain amount for a girl's wardrobe and then, when the season was about over, fired her and sold her outfit as new to the girl who took her place. Generally speaking, the girls were given enough weekly wage to pay for their room and board, plus about a dollar for spending money.

The girls led busy lives rehearsing, reporting for daily and often Sunday matinees, washing their own clothes. Friday nights they washed their tights so that they wouldn't have to carry them home on Sunday.

Tights were a great nuisance, yet a convenience also, as some of the girls wore them on the street to keep warm. It was not an unusual thing for girls on tour to convert the ladies' waitingroom in a railway station into an amateur laundry, with the windows serving as natural ironing boards for negligees.

Some of the girls in the show wore bustles, hip pads, symmetricals and what was the equivalent of the brassières of today.

Gus Hill, one of the most notoriously corrupt managers of the nineties, was a great champion for female decency. 'Our girls," he declared, "didn't show so much as a bare arm. They were covered up to their wrists and even if they did wear tights they were never flesh-colored, always some other color."

Ina Hayward was very proud of the fact that she was the first burlesque queen to wear a pair of lace tights. She saw a picture of them in a French magazine and promptly went home and made a similar pair — out of an old lace curtain.

When she wore them, however, the police came backstage and noticing that the small apertures between the lace exposed short areas of bare flesh, were about to arrest her. But she had been too smart for them. What looked like bare flesh was flesh-colored long underwear.

Living rates during the early days were seven dollars a week: three meals a day and a fourth meal at night with beer. Sometimes the hotel would ask three or four girls to share the same room. But the manager and his wife would get the best room in the house, for if he did not patronize the hotel, no one else did. The advance agent, or press agent, usually received board and room free.

Railway accommodations and theater facilities were always matters of contention. Out West, a certain theater was so small that it had but one dressing room for the entire company.

"Can't you put up a sheet?" begged one of the ladies of the manager. He looked astounded, then asked, "What's the matter with you folks? Ain't you speakin'?"

It is said that the gypping managers often met their match at the gallery entrance. Here the custodian in charge, the obscure ticket-taker, frequently ran a business of his own, admitting patrons at a sum lower than that charged at the box office, a sum that went straight into his own pocket.

Nor did a little misrepresentation trouble a manager if he thought it would bring money to the box office. The farther away he was from Broadway, the greater chances he could take.

Thus, the Broadway Belles Burlesque Company, on opening at Houston, Texas, was astonished when the curtain rose to find an audience of ladies and gentlemen in evening dress, diamonds and ermine, not knowing that the show had been advertised as the Broadway Extravaganza Company with Frankie

Bailey, the "Weber and Fields Star." Yet not even Frankie's legs, said to be the most beautiful in the world at that time, held the audience. For the elite of Houston, though beguiled by the advance advertisement, recognized a road burlesque show at sight. One by one, they left the theater; then in crowds; and by the time the curtain rose on the second act, the house was virtually empty.

Burlesque managers were in constant fear of police raids. Most of them had a system whereby their employees warned them, backstage or front, as to whether they should put on a "whore" show or keep things down. One or two managers, for their own security, went so far as to have special electric systems installed whereby red and green electric lights in the office or backstage announced the presence of a new police inspector or a city official.

Some companies played No. 1 and No. 2 shows, the first clean, the second dirty. If a policeman or censor came in, the manager would raise his hat several times, a warning to the comedian to clean up his jokes and simultaneously to the girls to eliminate "grinds" and "bumps." Some managers used buzzers to spread warnings backstage. Some spirited police officers off to the dressing rooms and the wings for drinks and introductions to the girls.

Yet with all these precautions there was many an actor who couldn't overcome his nervousness. One comedian who depended almost exclusively on raw material for his laughs, when warned that the police were going to observe his act grew so nervous that he almost collapsed. Happily, though, with the aid of strong drinks, the staff managed to get him to go on with the performance.

Producers advertised their shows with flamboyant posters showing girls' legs and garters. They sent out letters also which caused fights between wayward husbands and suspicious wives, letters that read:

> DEAR BOY:
>   Please meet me tonight at the stage door of the Gaiety
> Theatre at about 8:15. I'll be waiting for you.
> > With love,
> > VIOLET

Because of "come-ons" like this letter and, more important, indecent performances, burlesque companies were under constant police supervision, and a breach in conduct or a failure to respond to a political kickback often landed entire companies in jail.

The Golden Era—1900-1910

1900, the year when Sam Scribner organized the Columbia Circuit, saw the beginning of the golden age of burlesque. It reached its zenith with the opening of the Columbia Theatre in New York on January 6, 1910. This decade marked the heyday of burlesque, when entertainment was substantial and comedians robustious, starbound for Broadway. Managers were proud of their shows, flourished in their rivalry, introduced novelties, perfected book, score and production, made audiences happy. These were the days that middle-aged men now recall wistfully and that young men discuss boastfully; proud of the fact that during the glowing days of boyhood they had at least a glimpse of an entertainment which was man-sized.

Harry Morris, originally a Rentz-Santley player, furnished the impetus for the happy change in burlesque production which started with *Night on Broadway*, in 1902.

On a trip abroad with Sam Scribner, he attended a musical comedy in Berlin in which he saw possibilities for burlesque. He obtained the rights and had it adapted for American audiences. The story had a book, "The Three Hats," with a definite farcical plot. It made a hit, caused something of a managerial revolution. Thereupon, every manager began to busy himself with imitations, scrambling hither and thither for farces adaptable to burlesque. They also began looking for musical numbers since a hit song, "Hinky Dee," sung by Harry Morris, had an important part in the success of *Night on Broadway.*

Another powerful and continuous influence for the improvement of burlesque was the opening of the Weber and Fields Music Hall, where this form of entertainment, reattired under the title of travesty, created a new public and challenged producers with new ideas, new talent and new types of scenic investiture and display.

Thanks to the competition, the name of a manager on poster or program

Joe Welch, expert Yiddish dialect comic

"Bozo" Snyder invited gents in the audience to come up and dance with the ladies of the chorus

Modestly, this burlesquer es-
chews tights for bloomers

The Gayety,
a Washington temple
of burlesque

Ermines embellish tights

now became a kind of guarantee, indicating the type of entertainment and almost the exact nature and number of the laughs.

Bill Campbell's show, *Rose Sydell in the London Belles*, was moving on to its thirty years of satisfied service. Watson's *Beef Trust* with its immortal hefty dames was a yearly hit. Numerous were the enterprising managers: William "Biff" Clark and Peter S. Clark; Hyde and Behman; Hurtig and Seamon; Max Spiegel; Al Reeves, Campbell and Drew; Jacobs and Jarmon; Barney Gerard; Jack Singer; Fred Irwin. The mighty ones.

Will Rogers and Mrs. Winslow's Soothing Syrup headline leg-show program

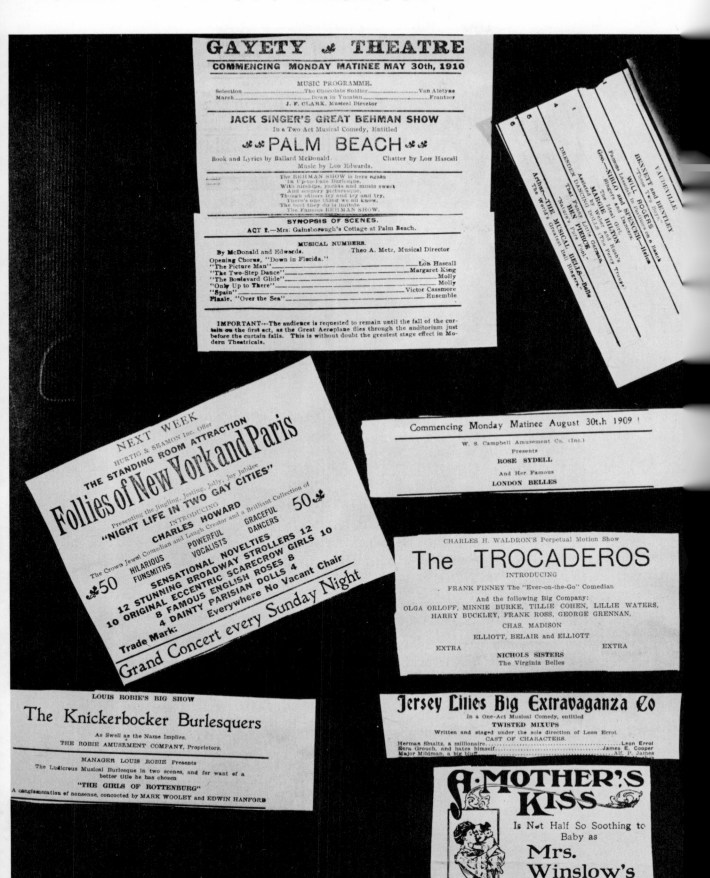

CULVER SERVICE

Ida Bayton, popular specimen of the perfect "principal boy,"
in *The Girls from Happyland*

Comics abounded — Ed Lee Wrothe, Harry Welsh, Harry Morris, Jack Pearl,
Loney Haskell, Bert Lahr, Bozo Snyder, Dave ('Snuffy the Cabman") Marion,
Ed Rush, George Sidney, Billy Arlington, Joe Welch, Ben Welch, Sam Howe,
Harry K. Morton, Tom Howard, Al Shean of Gallagher and Shean, Bickel and
Watson, and Ted Healy.

From 1904 to 1905 about forty shows were on the wheel, including Scribner's *Gay Moring's Show*, *The Bon Tons*, *The Imperials*, with Cliff Gordon,
Jack Singer's *Yankee Doodle Girls*, Rose Sydell's *London Belles*.

106

"Women's hidden charms," the burlesque come-on, are here properly
or improperly revealed from the
standpoint of realistic, abstract, or
what-have-you? art

Modern version of Amazon parade

When the wheels split into the Eastern and Western circuits in 1905 and 1906, managers intensified their efforts to provide new productions and playhouses. As a result, there were about seventy shows, with almost every house manager holding an interest in some traveling company. The Western route now included Spokane, San Francisco, Butte, Portland, Carson City, Reno, Ogden, and Salt Lake City, and extended from Duluth to the West Coast.

Stars in burlesque were something of a development. The names of women stars did often form part of the name of the company, but in some instances these names were imaginary. The real comedians, however, had to fight for recognition. In burlesque, the show was the thing and it took precedence. Thus the billing was first *The Golden Crook* with Billy Arlington, and later, perforce, Billy Arlington in *The Golden Crook*. Producers who owned the show, the franchise or part of it, could feature any name they wished.

108

Striptease

Burlesque, to the man who has never seen it, generally means just one thing: striptease. One of the unsolved mysteries of the theatrical world is who originated it. If conjecture is dependable this spectacle in terpischorean disrobing sprang, like Venus, full-blown from infinity.

Fleshly intimations of the oncoming striptease nudity were bared to the naked eye as far back as 1847. At that time Living Models or Tableaux Vivants drew audiences to at least five New York theaters where they were regaled with bare bodies and posturings that resembled the classic sculpture.

A Dr. Collyer was the original sponsor of these pseudo-aesthetic exhibits, and the participants included shapely women "without a blemish" and handsomely molded men, usually acrobats recruited from circuses.

The titles of the tableaux were descriptive of their intention and included

Living Models gladden the eyes and accelerate heartbeats

Entered according to act of Congress in the Year 1848, by J. Baillie, in the Clerk's Office of the District Court of the South.n Dist.t of N.Y.

THE THREE GRACES.
As exhibited by the MODEL ARTISTS of New-York.

Published by James Baillie, 87 th St near 3.d Avenue N.Y.

"The Three Graces," "Adam's First View of Eve" and "The Expulsion from Eden" — "scrupulous delineations in every detail to the original works."

These tableaux might have continued doing a lucrative business forever, had it not been for the advent of a new medium, the Free Love craze, which probably percolated through to the United States by way of France and the novels of George Sand.

This craze swept the country as did the subsequent Companionate Marriage fad, and usurped the halls of the living models. In their place, billboards carried announcements that the same lovely models would now serve as esoteric consultants, a racket which the police speedily terminated.

CULVER SERVICE

Early Living Models' prelude to Rodin's "The Kiss"

Ziegfeld version of the Living Models

Though the first series of ladies came to an ignominious end, the tribe bobbed up again from time to time. One manager offered "The Temple of the Muses" and "The Favorite of the Seraglio," and Mme. Pauline's troupe presented "The Rape of the Sabines."

At the conclusion of one performance, twenty living models appeared in a cotillion. To enjoy this *divertissement,* certain male enthusiasts came to the thea-

Mademoiselle Huton, who brought
nudity to the New World

Lustful looking

Adah Isaacs Menken lashed to a horse

ter "carrying," according to the critics, "prodigious opera glasses and pocket telescopes. The audience as a whole was made up of sensual old rakes, scoundrels around town and, yes, a few bankers and brokers."

In one instance, the gentlemen left their seats and jumped over the footlights, forcing the terrified models backstage and into their dressing rooms. Again the police locked the doors.

For a number of years after, living pictures continued as a feature of what was called the circus "concert," a brief variety entertainment, admission, ten cents. These models appeared on a circular platform surrounded by a circular

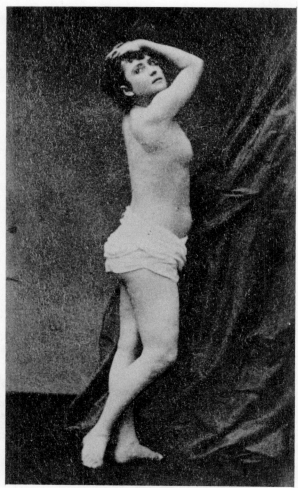

Adah Isaacs Menken unhorsed

Millie de Leon, the girl who threw away her garters

Charmaine broke her shoulder strap. Accidental?

curtain which, when drawn, showed men and women in "plastic poses," their hair covered with white wigs and their bodies with some sort of liquid that gave them the alabaster chastity of marble.

In 1893, the popular extravaganza *1492* revived the models in the legitimate theater. Gold-framed against a black background, the Kilanyi *tableaux vivants* were described by one critic as "by far the most beautiful arrangement of human beings ever seen in New York."

In the meantime man's Promethean effort to get a peek at what was once called "women's hidden charms" and "the secrets of the purdah" were being re-

Mary Garden as Salomé, engaged in unwinding herself from seven veils

Eva Tanguay's umbilical version of the Dance of the Seven Veils

warded in other theatrical directions. An early pioneer was Mlle. Francoise Hutin, supposedly a member of the Paris Opéra. Her debut took place at the Thalia Theatre in 1877.

Rumors concerning the "indelicacy of her costume and behavior" preceded her appearance, whetting the public appetite. And the members of the audience got what they expected, perhaps a little more.

Evaluating her performance, one reviewer wrote:

> At sight of her scanty drapery floating in air and her symmetrical proportions, liberally displayed, the cheeks of the greater portion of the audience were crimsoned with shame and every lady in the lower tier of boxes immediately left the house.

The next exponent of nudity managed to detain her audience, all male. Her name was Mme. Vestris (1797-1856) and she came to America fresh from triumphs in her native England and in France. Once arrived, she earned the title of "the first woman in modern times to teach burlesque to profit from the beauty of legs."

118

Sitting pretty

Gaby Deslys, first to introduce a striptease number in a Broadway musical

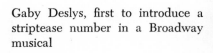

Mme. Vestris was a woman of many accomplishments. As a theatrical manager she set an example for decent and generous treatment of employees. She effected important changes in scenic design and found time also to appear before the footlights as a singer and dancer. Her specialty was "breeches" roles.

Her personal life was crowded with incident. After divorcing one husband, she fell in love with a prominent actor, Charles James Matthews, and created a great deal of excitement by announcing that before marrying him she would "tell all."

"What candor," remarked a member of her company while another cried, "What a memory!"

Another colorful episode had to do with her famous legs. In New York a young man was brought into custody, accused of the theft of her "legs," which had been stolen from a sculptor, the only person for whom Mme. Vestris had ever "stood." The legs had come into the possession of a shopkeeper who exhibited them in his window "in a shameful manner," the court was told, "thus causing Mme. Vestris great embarrassment."

The cause of nudity was carried a further step forward by Adah Isaacs Menken.

Lois De Fee, gigantesque stripper, gained national attention by a pseudo marriage to a midget

Ann Corio who, with Gypsy Rose Lee, was one of the first two important apostles of the striptease

"My kingdom for a horse!" cried Richard III. Unlike Richard, Adah Isaacs Menken had no kingdom, but she had a remarkable personality and also a horse.

At the age of thirteen when she started as a dancing girl in New Orleans, there was no indication of the colorful paragraph that she would write in the annals of the stage.

On the night of June 7, 1861, she displayed herself in tights, strapped to a living horse, in a play based on Byron's poem "Mazeppa." The feat created a sensation and resulted in a long run. Her act grew so popular that she had a score of imitators, including men who masqueraded as women.

Indefatigable in her interests, she went in for cigar smoking, women's rights and dress reform. She married. She left her husband. She wrote bad poetry and developed a penchant for fraternizing with authors. She made friends with Charles Reade, Walt Whitman, Mark Twain, Bret Harte, Dickens, Dante Gabriel Rossetti, Théophile Gautier and Alexander Dumas, père. Swinburne celebrated her personality in his poem, "Dolores."

The progress of nudity leveled off at this point. The first person to renew the art of undressing was Charmaine, a trapeze performer. Her procedure, however, was not intentional. She broke a shoulder strap during the performance, thereby causing an unexpected exposure of epidermis.

Deliberate, however, was the disarray of Millie de Leon. She didn't take off much, but what she did take off almost caused a riot in the theater. She removed her garter ostentatiously and then flung it over the footlights where the wolves rushed for it hungrily.

More extensive was the part that Mary Garden played in the art of undress. She was the greatest singing actress of her era and also the most proficient publicity hound. When she introduced the Richard Strauss opera *Salome* to the world she introduced also, and with justifiable appropriateness, the "Dance of the Seven Veils," which was much naughtier by implication than it was by pro-

Hal Skelly and girls in *Burlesque,* a play founded on the leg show

Faith Bacon, famous Ziegfeld figur-
ante

Claire Luce starred in London in
the hit play *Burlesque;* Barbara
Stanwyck created the role at the
New York premiére (1926)

Grateful glimpses of striptease denuding

In the sacred privacy of their dressing room the peelers prepare to undress

cedure. Olive Fremstad did the same dance, expurgated, at the Metropolitan Opera House.

Nevertheless the *divertissement* caused so much excitement that the clergy declared against it, whereupon the public promptly rushed to see it.

The dance started a Salome craze which enlisted the talents of Gertrude Hoffman and Eva Tanguay, the "I Don't Care Girl," who concluded this musical declaration of independence by pouring a bottle of champagne over her tousled hair.

Other runners-up for striptease distinction were Theda Bara who did the "Dance of the Seven Veils" in the early movies. The famous French music hall star, Gaby Delys, perhaps without realizing the importance of her accomplishment, was the first actress to present the striptease in a Broadway show. She recited these lines by Irving Berlin in *Stop, Look and Listen* (1915) while removing articles of apparel:

> "Take off a little bit.
> If that don't make a hit,
> Take off a little bit more.
> Take off a little bit.
> Don't let it drag on the floor.
> The doctor, the lawyer, the Indian Chief,
> Will always look longer
> When dresses are brief.
> Take off a little bit.
> If that don't make a hit,
> Take off a little bit more."

125

One of the best-known modern peelers, Lili St. Cyr

Margie Hart
looking spiritual

FAUER

Bonnie Kerr

The two "artistes" — the swank term gradually adopted by strippers — who did most to popularize the number and accustom the public to the shock implicit were Ann Corio and Gypsy Rose Lee. As a result of their distinctive contributions to the development of striptease, the word "artiste" was soon abandoned in favor of the more accurate "stripper" and "peeler." Some ladies, however, called themselves "ecdysiasts," a cultural appellation derived from the word "ecdysis," meaning "molting" or "shedding."

As pursued by Gypsy and Ann, the art of undressing became a ceremony with a special technique and nomenclature. The number itself was a combination of posing, strutting, dancing and singing punctuated from time to time by thrusts and twists of the abdomen called "bumps" and "grinds."

The various steps were known in succession as the "flash" or entrance, the "parade," or the march across the stage in full costume; the "tease," or increasing removal of wearing apparel while the audience, lusting for bed and body, shouted, "Take 'em off. Take 'em off. More. More"; and the climactic strip or denuding down to the G-string, followed by a speedy retreat into the obscuring draperies before the police could move in.

There were, of course, individualistic changes in this routine. Some dancers dyed their hair a special color so that it would show better under the spotlight. There were also elaborate varieties of the G-string, the stripteaser's substitute for the classic fig leaf of statuary. Some were decorated with paste jewels, others contained an electric bulb which could be flashed off and on at will.

At first each show had only one striptease dancer. Then opposition managers

Gypsy furnishes a peek at the area between garter and panties

Grandiose Gypsy Rose Lee, realized dream of stripper perfection

Though prim in mood and manner, Sherry Britton
can shed her habiliments quickly for a change of pace

PHOTO BY JEANNE AND JERRY SAGER, COURTESY LEE MORTIMER

Rose La Rose, convolution champion

BRUNO

Carmen Bridges

began increasing the number until the Minskys, with their customary prodigality, exhibited a whole stageful of young ladies with both breasts bare and nude down to the umbilical cord.

Finally, nudity reached the point where it all but took over the whole show. The result was the demise of the comedy element, which had been burlesque's rich contribution to the art of the theater.

Meanwhile striptease had become a household word. Society women were doing it at charity bazaars. The number broke into Broadway by way of *Pal Joey* and also through a delightful take-off performed by Imogene Coca, who didn't take off a thing. Fifty-second Street was the mecca for the undressers where all kinds of new names came up in electric lights and all sorts of costumes came down in muffled lights and shadows. And some of the hardiest wriggled and bumped for half an hour at a time.

Kim Stanley brought the striptease to the legitimate stage in *Bus Stop*

Gwen Verdon in *Damn Yankees* added dynamics to the striptease

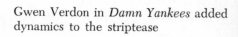

No sooner had the art of dishabille caught the public fancy than a swarm of new experts demanded attention for their fresh contributions to the art.

Margie Hart was an early exponent of adroit exposure as was Sherry Britton, who now slips occasionally into legitimate roles. Lily St. Cyr is a name with which to conjure and Rose La Rose someone to marvel over, for she claims a record for the numbers of umbilical "convolutions" that she can negotiate in a given number of seconds.

Francesca, the Bombshell

TRIXIE ROGERS

Today, according to veteran reporter Charlie Uno, a thousand stripteasers are employed in night clubs and burlesque houses, some of which still subject the artistes to the ignominy of the hook.

Some of the recent peelers have discarded their real personalities for trick names which excite the imagination, making the advertisements colorful and more suggestive. This list includes Jan Tiffany, the Jewel of Broadway; Ann Tenna; Apple Pie, the All-American Dish; Peppy Cola; Venus la Doll; Bonnie Bell, the Ding Dong Girl; and Alky Seltzer, the Bumps and Burps Girl.

Gradually burlesque and striptease seeped through to formal Broadway. It is now a familiar ingredient in musical comedy and legitimate drama.

Pat "Amber" Halladay

Val de Val

Jeanne Adair, the Mystery Girl

Eunice Jason

Kim Stanley used the medium as a serious motif in *Bus Stop*. Tamara Geva did a striptease in *On Your Toes*. The most sensational interpretation, outdoing every conceivable creation of the past, was Gwen Verdon's in *Damn Yankees*.

Of the plays using burlesque as a theme, *The Naked Truth*, by the famous stripteaser Gypsy Rose Lee, had a brief run at the Plymouth Theatre. *Top Banana*, a musical with Phil Silvers, famous burlesquer, had a long run at the Winter Garden. *Strip for Action*, by Lindsay and Crouse, played at the National.

But the most important play about the leg show was *Burlesque* written by Arthur Hopkins and George Manker Watters. With Hal Skelly, Barbara Stanwyck made her first important hit in this long-run piece and then appeared in the motion picture *The Lady of Burlesque* which was based on the mystery novel *The G-String Murders* by Gypsy Rose Lee.

Claire Luce starred in the English production of *Burlesque*, becoming the idol of London after having already won the admiration of Paris where she followed Mistinguette, who possessed the most famous legs in the world.

Nudity reached its pinnacle in *The Women,* by Clare Booth Luce, when one of the ladies of the cast took a bath in full view of the audience, an intrusion on personal privacy that millions shared when the play was translated to the screen.

Striptease spread to London in 1940 and then made a belated debut in Paris about 1954, a revolutionary reversal in procedure in a city noted for nudity, a reversal noted recently in this French revue bit:

BRUNO

Sally Keith, Tassel Twirler

Irma the Body

Virginia Kinn, the White Orchid

Sally Lane and her monkey, Fifi

Princess La Homa

Following their marriage, a bride and groom enter the nuptial chamber almost nude, but show no interest in each other. Then the bride puts on her stockings and the groom his socks. Immediately their desires are inflamed and by the time that they are fully clothed, passion is rampant.

But it remained for a one-woman battalion named Carrie Fennell to destroy all the sensuous and sexy implication of bare breasts that had persisted for centuries. Before the astonished eyes of the audience she made her breasts pop up

Cynthia the Silhouette

Mia Lynn

Honey Michel

and down, vibrate, sizzle and fume. From that moment on, the aesthetic glory that started with Venus and continued through a million embattled dressmakers faded out.

If burlesque audiences were shocked by the exposure of female bosoms and bare legs, they would have been more shocked, doubtless, to discover that the American public has made a complete turnabout and is now concentrating on the hairy chest of the male.

Marlon Brando initiated the mode, Ralph Meeker brought it to the stage in

MURRAY KORMAN

Georgia Sothern

Lily Christine,
the Cat Girl

MURRAY KORMAN

Picnic, and Mae West, always an addict of the superlative, brought near-nude escorts to the night club. Now television, motion pictures and amusement ads all exploit the upper part of the male form.

Whether or not the present casual acceptance of the frank exposure of the human body is a social loss or gain is something which the individual must determine for himself and the sociologist will eventually appraise. The current emphasis, nurtured by actors, directors, press agents and advertising agencies, seems to be esoteric rather than aesthetic. Sex, however, has always been one of the chief considerations of the arts and a continuous influence in the growth of civilization.

Burlesque is an outcast entertainment today. Swarms of strippers dominate what is left of it. They have crowded out the comics, who are now merely fillers between one undressing and another, stopgaps between wrigglings and bumps. Professional members of the burlesque business rate the shows "N. T. and T." No talent and "tits."

Mae West invites an Apollo to come up and see her sometime

These are days when universal peace is menaced by the hydrogen bomb. Yet who takes time out to ponder world conditions? The emphasis is on cheesecake. Let an empress arrive in America, a humanitarian or a scientist, the first thing the lady must do is show her legs. Marilyn Monroe with her skirt in the air captures the eyes of millions.

Marilyn Monroe, international MM-body-ment of the cheesecake era. In the film *Show Business* she did bumps and grinds.

14

Books and Music

For the most part, the librettos or books for burlesque shows had little worth or distinction. A few, however, were highly successful and were even turned later into legitimate productions.

The most successful book ever written for an American burlesque show was *Me, Him and I*, by Willard Holcombe, who always claimed that the word "ho-kum" derived from his name. It was originally written in 1901 as a two-act piece entitled *On the Yu-con*, with an olio in between. The next year Holcombe added an extra act in which, probably for the first time on any stage, an airplane was introduced. The scene showed three bums who are trying to beat their way to the Yukon aboard a yacht. The yacht steams off without them, where-upon they steal an airplane. Just as the plane, which was suspended on wires, overtakes the yacht, it runs out of gas and falls onto the deck of the yacht. The stunt caused a sensation and the show became the most popular thing in bur-lesque. As a result, it was turned into a musical comedy. Holcombe rewrote it, introducing a love story and changing the title to *Me, Him and I*. Max Hoffman wrote the score. It played seven years, elevated Bickel, a cornetist, and Watson, a pantomimist, to top-flight comedians, and produced a hit song, "Harry, Harry, Won't You Marry Me?" which Gertrude Hoffman sang with a couple of six-shooters pointed at the boys in the boxes.

The first burlesque show to draw a class audience of both sexes was *Chuckles*, with Clark and McCullough. But previous to this, *Wine, Women and Song*, 1905, drew evening-dress slumming parties, the Four Hundred riding up in victorias.

This show had a unique history. It started as a road burlesque and ended as a legitimate production, playing legitimate houses only.

The cast originated in an excellent burlesque show called *Casino Girls in Smiling Island*. The show itself took form in an incredible manner. The principals ad libbed most of the dialogue and contributed their own bits, then directed themselves while a dancer in the company put on the numbers.

Wine, Women and Song opened at the Dewey on Fourteenth Street, struck the fancy of the public immediately, and moved, first to Miner's Bowery and later to Miner's Eighth Avenue.

As the show was about to end its successful run something extraordinary happened. The Circle Theatre on Broadway had just been remodeled and the new managers, having watched the progress of the show, decided to take a chance on a four-week booking — a highly hazardous arrangement, considering the fact that a burlesque show had never before been deliberately offered to the Broadway public.

Immediately the members of the company began betting that they wouldn't last three weeks. But *Wine, Women and Song* lasted a year and a half.

The first act opened with a masque ball on the lawn of the Asterbilt estate at Newport, at which the guests were supposed to come as Broadway stars, dressed in their regular stage make-up. Alexander Carr came as David Warfield; Bonita, first as Miss Asterbilt, then as Lillian Russell; Orville Harrold as Caruso. Part of the success was due to these imitations, the first, it is said, to be introduced into a Broadway show.

Imitations soon became the rage. Seats worth two dollars got fifty from the speculators — an unprecedented occurrence in the history of burlesque. The entertainment was clean, and original. The company had ad libbed together so long that the gags were set, the punch lines certain, and the comedy smooth. The girls appeared only once in tights, in the Amazon parade finale to the first act. There was no set score, just a collection of popular numbers sung by the principals and chorus.

Topical events quickly introduced into the show were the talk and delight of Broadway and helped to prolong the run.

About this time Caruso was caught in the monkey house at the zoo, flirting with a woman. It was a national scandal, on every front page. The episode was immediately incorporated into the show. A great gate with bars across it was set up on the estate scene and Orville Harrold came out and sang "Pagliacci." As he did so Lew Hearn, dressed up as a sheriff, with a silver star in his hat and a Prince Albert goatee, began pacing up and down behind the bars. The business was improvised and accidental, but it took the house by storm.

With Byronic speed, *Wine, Women and Song* made Bonita famous overnight. In addition to impersonating Lillian Russell, she posed as the Gibson girl and was the first woman to wear a sheath gown. This stunt in itself created a miniature riot among patrons, who stormed the matinees for photographs.

However, the outstanding hit of the performance was Alexander Carr's number called "Toblitzsky Says," a character study that established his fame, took him to London and made him an unforgettable figure in American theatrical history. Meanwhile Orville Harrold became a star at the "Met."

Though burlesque served as a perfect school for comedians, it did little for the lyric writer and composer. As the audience paid slight attention to the score, managers didn't waste money on buying fresh compositions. One manager, completely indifferent to authorship, headed his program with the announcement: "Musical numbers by J. H. Remick Co."

As a result, what corresponded to a burlesque musical score was just so much necessary filler between bits, hootch dances, strip numbers and variety. It was these last features which brought money to the box office, not the ingenuity of ensembles, finales, solos and orchestrations. Every audience expected popular ballads, of course, but the managers got these for nothing.

To place a ballad, however, in a burlesque show was the infallible method, in the nineties and long afterward, of establishing a hit and insuring great profits. The runs were long, and by the time one show after another presented a song the whole country knew the tune by heart. Thus composers and song publishers went to great lengths to place their numbers and displace competitors.

Assemblage of comics in *Wine, Women and Song*

Orville Harrold in *Wine, Women and Song.* He went from burlesque to the Met.

A song in a burlesque show represented a potential fortune and the time soon came when publishers were willing to spend money. They sent out their pluggers to burlesque rehearsals to play numbers and induce managers to use them. Then these song pluggers would stage the numbers free of charge or teach the musical director how to put them on. And finally, in order to intensify the force of a song, the publishers began to spend real money. They would dress a number. If there were lilacs in the lyrics they'd pay for putting artificial ones into the scene. The time came when publishers even paid vaudeville people a weekly amount for putting over a number.

According to George Gershwin, burlesque made a notable contribution to music in the person of Frank Sadler, the father of modern arranging. From a leader of burlesque orchestras Sadler rose to professional arranger, responsible for arranging all the early works of Jerome Kern and such hits as *Oh Boy*. His method broke so sharply with tradition that he can be said to have started a completely new school.

J. Fred Coots deserves mention here also, for he attracted the attention of Barney Gerard and wrote for him the popular score for *Follies of the Day*. Harry Archer, composer of the all-time favorite "I Love You," from *Little Jesse James*, wrote a number of worthy scores.

But if burlesque had only a scattered influence on native composers, it had much to do with the inception of jazz, generally considered America's foremost contribution to the art world. This fresh native form of musical expression

150

had a disputed course, with either St. Louis or New Orleans its first focal points up to 1917, and subsequently Chicago, with the emergence of Louis "Satchmo" Armstrong. Recently, under the leadership of the remarkable Armstrong, jazz has become a powerful medium for exploiting democracy throughout a great part of the world.

Yet jazz, the "sinful" side of music, was held in contempt by the musical American highbrow until Paul Whiteman presented Gershwin's *Rhapsody in Blue,* at Aeolian Hall (1924). But, up to then, the "Europeans were writing about it," notes J. S. Wilson, "and forming clubs where it could be heard and discussed in the nineteen twenties, at a time when jazz was still limited largely to honkytonks and the seamier deadfalls in its native land."

Irving Berlin, the "jazz bombshell," set off the spark of ragtime about 1913. His early composition "Alexander's Ragtime Band," more than any other single number, was responsible for popularizing this idiom. As a young composer, he personally plugged this song in burlesque houses and taught the directors how to present it. The song was first introduced as an interpolated number in *Merry Whirl,* a production sponsored by Gordon and North, staged by Ben Teal, with book by Aaron Hoffman, lyrics by Edward Madden and score by Leo Edwards.

Irving Berlin's career is a magnificent example of the American way. He started life as a singing waiter and became one of the outstanding composers of popular songs and musical comedy. One of his best-beloved songs was written for the Follies, "A Pretty Girl Is Like a Melody." Berlin married Ellen Mackay, a successful author and daughter of Clarence Mackay, president of the Pacific Telegraph Company.

He wrote the most popular song of the First World War, "Oh, How I Hate To Get Up in the Morning." Recently the composer received a medal which read: Presented to Irving Berlin by President Eisenhower in national recognition and appreciation of his service in composing many patriotic songs, including 'God Bless America.'"

Burlesque, directly or indirectly, fostered Williams and Walker, honky-tonk graduates who popularized the cakewalk; and gave full opportunity for the development of Gershwin in such later colored musical comedies as *Shuffle Along, Strut Miss Lizzie* and *Black Birds,* happy media for artistic expression for Ethel Waters, Bill Robinson and other distinguished colored performers.

In 1896 *The Black Patti Troubadors* made a great financial success, with Sisseretti Jones as Black Patti. This gifted singer anticipated a later graduate of colored burlesque, Florence Mills, greatest colored musical comedy artist of our own times.

Among the other lyricists, librettists and composers who contributed to burlesque were Earl Carroll, the producer, who worked for Jack Singer for fifty dollars per week; the prolific Joe E. Brown, Ballard MacDonald, Edward Moran, Lon Haskell, Sam Howe, Seymour Furth and the able Negro composers, Henry S. Creamer and Will H. Vodery.

Irving Berlin, singing waiter at
Nigger Mike's, graduate *summa
cum laude*

Joe Howard, minstrel man and
composer, who had more wives
than Bluebeard

Burlesque also furnished the occasion for many interesting commercial and musical innovations. It was in burlesque, for instance, that the fad for singing in the gallery took impetus, the first singer of this type being Gus Edwards, who was to provide the stage and screen through discovery, presentation, and development with some of its finest talent — a theatrical entrepreneur who had much to do with the early recognition of such important artists as Eddie Cantor, George Jessel, Georgie Price, Eddie Buzzel, Hildegarde, Walter Winchell and scores of lesser figures.

Not content with presenting the public with so much talent, Mr. Edwards simultaneously provided material for this talent: acts and songs, some of the biggest popular hits of the period, including the famous

> School days, school days,
> Dear old golden-rule days . . .

Popular songwriters like Gus Edwards and Joe E. Howard had an important influence on burlesque. If a song pleased an audience, the audience whistled the tune and carried it out to the world where it eventually took root in the home. For in those days almost every home had a piano and the favorite form of home entertainment was standing around that piano and singing songs.

"Lucky Joe" was the title attached to Howard because of his phenomenal success as an actor, composer, singer, writer, producer of musicals and lady killer. Born in 1867, he grew into a handsome tenor who was singing high, pure notes in his seventies.

The son of a saloonkeeper, Joe, at the age of eight, ran away from home after the death of his mother. He found a new home in a Catholic orphanage where he delayed several years, only to break away again to seek his fortune in the West.

At Kansas City he joined McNeak, Johnson and Slavin's Minstrels on almost the same day that little Bobby Ford was being tried for the murder of Jesse James. Once started on a professional career, Joe began turning out songs that millions have sung and are still singing, including "What's the Use of Dreaming?" "Hello, My Baby," and "I Wonder Who's Kissing Her Now," which Howard "rendered," at the last count, 760,000 times.

Almost as successful as Joe E. Howard was another song writer of the same era, Harry Von Tilzer, who is said to have added the "von" to give distinction to what he considered a commonplace name.

In every home also, on every piano rack, was a picture of Harry Von Tilzer, for this composer of popular songs, runner-up for Joe E. Howard's totals, was the first song writer to place his picture on a sheet of music.

He wrote more than three thousand songs, including such favorites as "Wait Till the Sun Shines, Nellie," "What You Goin' To Do When the Rent Comes 'Round?" and "A Bird in a Gilded Cage," which rivaled "After the Ball" for sentimental appeal.

15

Burlesque Stars on Broadway

Though a number of burlesquers came to Broadway, just how they reached the magic street is usually a mystery. Willie Howard, Eddie Cantor, George Jessel and other famous stars had great talents which entitled them to the highest recognition, but most of them started so young in burleycue, honky-tonk, dime museum, beer garden and variety that little is known of their early service.

Some of them took part in elemental comedy acts like Eddie Cantor, who used a different name as a boy performer. Al Jolson peddled water in the gallery and sang songs in the aisles. Fred Stone and Will Rogers appeared in the

Gus Edwards (center) in an early production of his famous *Schooldays* tabloid

olio, a midway variety program. A score of youngsters made up the ensembles of Gus Edwards' *School Days*. Lew Hearn, one of the popular comics, declared that the burlesque afterpiece gave raw recruits their training because they had to read lines and play all sorts of parts.

But whatever chores the stars of later days performed in burlesque, most of them strove to conceal their association with the outcast entertainment. So it is almost impossible to discover what they did. More important, however, is the fact, that having received that early training, they were able to develop their latent abilities and develop new ones. The play often forces the player to make the most of himself. And the burlesquers who came to Broadway were tops.

But how did they get their start?

How could boys from ten to fourteen years of age become the early stars of burlesque and develop into the great comics who entertained the nation for decades?

The answer is that most of them went to a preparatory school, where they learned the basic principle of singing, dancing and timing before registering in the rigorous college of comedy-burlesque.

The school was situated at 28th Street between Broadway and Sixth Avenue.

Gus Edwards' *Schooldays* and *Kid Kabaret* tabloids were the burgeoning spots for young talent. The pupils here include George Jessel (left) and Eddie Cantor (center)

Joe Fields tells Lew Weber a few facts about nothing at all

It was adjacent to Proctor's Fifth Avenue's vaudeville house and with the exception of a large restaurant — Mouquin's — occupied an entire city block.

The school policy was unusual. There were no entrance examinations. All that the pupils required was an appetite for money and a latent talent or genius. Also, they had to be stage-struck.

There were no entrance requirements and no tuition fees, because the school subsisted on the returns of song-plugging which at that time, fifty years ago, was a major amusement industry.

The name of the school was Tin Pan Alley and it was composed of a series of music publishing houses all contiguous to each other.

156

The faculty was made up of song pluggers, rehearsal pianists and composers. Prominent among the composers was Ted Snyder, who wrote "The Sheik of Araby," and Ernest R. Ball, who wrote "Love Me and the World Is Mine."

These specialists gave daily instruction in how to put over a new song to most of the professional entertainers of that era: Marie Cahill, Hattie Williams, Chauncey Olcott, Mae Irwin, Eva Tanguay, Irene Franklin, Jack Norworth and Charlie King, later featured in the Ziegfeld Follies and George M. Cohan musicals.

Fortunately while this intensified instruction was in progress the windows of the song studios were wide open and the tunes percolated through to the elementary class, the small fry stationed on the sidewalk: Willie and Eugene Howard, Don Barclay, Dan Healy, Bert Gordon, the "Mad Russian," Eddie Cantor and subsequently George White, producer of the Scandals.

Never were the members of a class more attentive. They were all ears. Meticulously, they learned the tunes as they listened, imitated every inflection of the words and music.

In order to enter the next class and learn another lesson — a new song number — all a pupil had to do was to stand under another open window and listen again attentively. Then he would scurry off to the nearest barroom, beer garden or honky-tonk.

One of the greatest comics of burlesque, musical comedy and revue was Willie Howard, star of half a century

Once inside, he would proceed to sing the songs until someone yelled "Shut up!" or "Kick the kid out!" But just as often, a kindly bartender or a friendly drunk would come to the rescue, shouting, "Give the kid a chance! Let's hear him."

Thus encouraged, the young entertainer would resume his vocalizing and, if the applause was hearty, he would pass the hat. Usually the coins dropped in and encores followed.

Sometimes, however, a wily bartender, hearing the clinking, would demand a kickback, refusing to let the singer return unless he split the returns. The kid had to consent, of course, but he soon learned to hold back a few coins by slipping them underneath the lining of his cap.

Day after day and night after night, after curfew hours, the kids ran from one night spot to another, sometimes making as many as twenty appearances. And as they ran hither and thither, they carried concealed amusement impedimenta in their back pockets — split clogs. Like regular clogs, these adjuncts to fancy stepping were made of wood but were split in the middle and had a leather instep. They cost three dollars a pair.

Soon the kids' shenanigans took on an unexpected importance. The music publishers, recognizing their potential commercial importance, began to engage

"Diamond Jim" Brady, theatergoer and bon vivant

Lillian Russell, the "American Beauty," revue and variety star who married Ambassador Alexander Moore. Her favorite escort was "Diamond Jim" Brady

W. C. Fields, bulbous-nosed in
typical comic costume

Bobby Clark with his cane,
cigar, and phony glasses

them to sing through microphones at the old Madison Square Garden before the fight audiences, a service for which they received one dollar a night.

On the strength of this recognition, a few dared to go directly to the publishers' offices and ask for professional copies of new songs. And because they were known in that concentrated bistro-entertainment orbit, they received, instead of a rebuff, free copies of the music they requested.

The next recognition was far more dignified and profitable. It lifted the kid from the bistro miraculously into what was once an imposing part of theater architecture — a stage box. For news travels fast in the amusement world and when word got around that a certain youngster had a high soprano voice and could put a song over, an enterprising manager engaged him to sing from the box and over the footlights to and with the star of the show.

It was a surprise novelty and Anna Held was once one of the first to pair off with a kid, a stunt which Ethel Merman duplicated years after in *Call Me Madam*, when she walked on the stage and duetted with a little girl about eight years of age.

The current revival of song plugging with child aides and other stunts has been developed through the sale of records which pyramids to the millions and requires that singers make personal appearances, cater to disc jockeys and help increase juke-box sales, a procedure which the gangsters are striving to take over.

Fifty years ago, ragamuffin child entertainers were called "buskers" and their vagabond-minstrelsy "busking," a vulgarized derivative of the classic term *buskin*, the sandal which the tragic Greek actor wore to increase his height.

When these buskers grew a little older they were ready for the next step toward polishing for a professional entrance into burlesque — appearances at amateur nights. The rest of their history branches off here into the story of the individual stars.

Some of the greatest dramatic actors of the day played in burlesque. They gained their training through appearing in the afterpiece and playing all sorts of roles under pressure.

The actors got their lines on Thursday, and Monday night they had to play them. Rehearsals began early Monday morning. The actors would rehearse and play all day, eat supper and then go straight on with the show.

Though the young burlesquers of the nineties escaped the frightful slashing that Chicago gangsters inflicted on the lovable comic of this era, Joe E. Lewis, they were at the mercy of minor gangsters, certain cruel and avaricious managers. Yet hunger and a precocious faith in their latent genius made them capable somehow of carrying on.

The story of their hardships is alternately incredible, pathetic and heart-warming. This generalization is poignantly true of most of the great laughmakers of the last fifty years, particularly of W. C. Fields, Eugene and Willie Howard, Dave Montgomery, Fred Stone, Bobby Clark, and Weber and Fields.

As mere children, Joe Weber and Lew Fields started their arduous efforts to

"Banjo eyes," Eddie Cantor's laughter directive

earn a living, outwit crafty managers and develop their natural comedy gifts.

The mingled reminiscences of Weber and Fields are involved with the early production of May Howard in *Night Owls* and with Sam Bernard and the Rentz-Santley company. But they got their start in the rough and tumble of dime museums, honky-tonks and music halls.

Weber (1867-1942) and Fields (1867-1941) grew to be Broadway stars of first importance, and producers of elegant burlesques entitled *Twirly-Whirly*, *Whoop-Dee-Doo*, *Hoity-Toity* and *Higgledy-Piggledy*. Their most famous star was Lillian Russell, "The American Beauty," who was squired by "Diamond Jim" Brady and married, among others, Alexander Moore, Ambassador to Spain. Lew produced, separately, hits like *A Connecticut Yankee*, starring William Gaxton, and *Hit the Deck*.

"Help, Help!" was the cry that had an important part at the beginning of W. C. Fields' career. The scene of this emergency plea was a beer garden called the Fortescue Pavilion, in Atlantic City. Here the management offered entertainment, free of charge. Patrons simply paid five cents for a glass of beer and the sales of this amber beverage helped take care of running expenses.

Generally business was pretty good. But any time it showed signs of falling off, the solution was to drown ten-year-old Fields. The method, though simple, required his full co-operation.

All he had to do was to swim some distance out into the ocean, shout "Help!"

162

Al Reeves, who picked the banjo and beautiful burlesquers

Genuflecting while raising his hands heavenward and shouting "Mammy!" was Al Jolson's "monogram"

Anna Held could manage her body but she "couldn't make her eyes behave." She sang with a kid in the gallery

MUSEUM OF THE CITY OF NEW YORK

then dive under the water and come up after a minute, repeating the same cry. Then, apparently aroused by the danger of the situation, two or three "plants" on the shore swam out and faked a rescue while innocent bystanders shouted, "Someone's drowning."

Immediately a crowd began to collect, but by this time the phony rescuers were carrying back young Fields, who was spitting water copiously, sometimes straight into the faces of the bystanders.

Once back in the pavilion, the men would throw Fields across a table and begin applying all the approved methods of artificial respiration.

At this moment the band would play, the Irish comedian would walk out on the stage and the attention of the crowd would be diverted. Some would take seats and order beer. Others would walk away indifferently, the boy completely forgotten.

For his nautical services, Fields received ten dollars a week with room and board, each equally inferior.

The subsequent career of this great artist was precarious, varied and almost incredible. He traveled through Europe as a juggler and on his return, some years later, turned from a juggler into a comedian. He became a star of the Ziegfeld Follies and also one of the most famous and highest paid screen actors.

"Adequate" was the critical estimate of Bobby Clark's first professional appearance as an entertainer. His engagement ran for one week as one of the features of the annual Elk's Circus. He must have been about fourteen years old at the time and he was already teamed up with Paul McCullough, who was four years older.

The sensational climax of their performance was to have been a back-flip with Bobby landing on McCullough's shoulders. Instead, Bobby landed in a tub of pink lemonade.

This misadventure did not lessen his ambition. At sixteen, he and McCullough joined the Culhane, Chase and Weston Minstrels. Their assignment included a blackface specialty, barrel-jumping, tumbling, horizontal bar acrobatics, a soft-shoe shuffle and appearing in the afterpiece.

They played the South until the show broke up; then joined one troupe after another, robbed of their salaries time after time yet carrying on miraculously and developing their comedy powers.

With their eventual appearance in burlesque they were for many years popular favorites, lauded for their rare foiling.

After the passing of McCullough, Bobby won admittance into the formal world of Broadway where his arrogant insouciance, phony spectacles, perpetual cigar and swanky cane soon made him an outstanding star of musical comedy.

From musical comedy he turned to cinema. His great triumphs came, however, with his assumption of comedy roles on the legitimate stage, including such classic fare as Sheridan's *The Rivals* and Moliere's *Bourgeois Gentilhomme.* For his artistry in this last difficult role, John Chapman, critic of the *News,* awarded him the recognition that marks the apogee of a burlesquer's achievement: "If Bobby Clark would just learn French, he would fit right into the Comédie Francaise, at least in *The Bourgeois Gentilhomme.*"

Fred Stone's life was influenced by a traveling mountebank who came through town and did a wire-walking stunt which so impressed Fred that he went home and started to learn the same tricks. He set up chairs and ladders in the back yard and, with the help of his younger brother Eddie, finally acquired great skill at an impressive height.

When a circus came to town he applied to the management for a job as a wire walker. The management tried him out on a wire that was perilously high. Fred walked steadily and safely, however, attributing his success to the fact that he never looked down. The management immediately signed up the two Stone brothers, Fred being eleven and Eddie nine.

Their father, a fatuous stage-struck barber, allowed the boys to join the circus with the understanding that they be properly cared for. They were to share quarters with the other members of the troupe in a decent hotel and have wholesome food and good clothes. Once out of town, however, the crafty circus manager retired to his comfortable hotel room and left the boys on the lot. Terrified by the sounds of the wild animals, they crawled under a tent and slept on the hay-strewn ground. For days and weeks they went without proper food, their clothing vermin-infested. They wrote to their father begging for help, but the management intercepted their letters. Finally the townsfolk and police authorities, noting their plight, came to their aid and sent them back home.

Fred went on from one form of amusement to another, finally getting a brief engagement in the olio of a burleycue.

Out of this beginning grew the talented comedian and the unparalleled dancer, the beloved teammate of David Montgomery who enchanted young-

Jimmy Savo and Margie Hart caught in an unconventional circumstance

sters and oldsters in *The Wizard of Oz, The Red Mill* and other great musical comedies.

Though the son didn't take his father's name, the name of Yule was popular in Western burlesque, particularly at the Follies Theatre where Joe Yule was a comic for twenty-two years. His stage career began when he was a child performer in old-fashioned melodramas like *The Slaves of New York* and *The Volunteer Organist*.

In 1932 he started his burlesque stretch, and if the actor who played the role of Finian in *Finian's Rainbow* hadn't left the cast, New Yorkers would never have had a chance to see the ingratiating characterization presented by Joe Yule, Sr. His son, however, they had seen in person many times and in many pictures, for Joe Yule, Jr., is known as Mickey Rooney.

Eddie Cantor started his burlesque engagements with Frank B. Carr's show and worked later with Jean Bedini, one of burlesque's greatest producers. In these brief appearances he set the scales for a magnificent career that has made him what is called a "perennial star" of every form of light entertainment.

His Broadway hits include the Ziegfeld Follies and *Kid Boots*. His flair for comedy is irrepressible. He is more than a comedian because he is never limited to his lines. His ability to see a comic situation as a whole has made him an invaluable participant in the shaping of musical comedies, revue, black-outs and television sketches.

Al Jolson's trademark — dropping suddenly to his knees, stretching out his arms imploringly, looking up to the heavens and crying "Mammy!" — was infringed upon thousands of times by imitators and impersonators.

Star of one successful Shubert musical after another, Al Jolson was an ideal minstrel man, a glorified replica of the old banjo-singing Negro. He loved to entertain and his famous "You ain't heard nothing yet" was a self-starter for innumerable encores.

Al's first job was selling water in the gallery of Eddie Herman's burlesque show at one cent a glass. He started show business with Al Reeves in Washington. The son of a Jewish cantor, who began making money by selling newspapers, he often sang as he walked up and down the streets. Herman brought the boy to Reeves' attention, with the result that Reeves engaged him to join the company. Whereupon Jolson left home at the age of fifteen.

First he sold songbooks, singing as he went up and down the aisles of the theater. Then he sang with two girls named Celeste and Batiste who did a sister act. One day he saw Celeste smoking a cigarette. He'd never seen a woman smoke before, and he was so heartbroken he wept.

Through his introduction of songs in *The Jazz Singer*, the first talking film, Jolson made singing an integral part of motion pictures.

"King of Burlesque" was the title that an adoring public bestowed on Al Reeves. But this hard-won appellation was not enough to satisfy his grandiose ambitions. Like other burlesquers he patterned himself on legitimate theater

The Rogers Brothers, who deserted burlesque for musicals with geographical tags

elegance. He called himself "The John Drew of Burlesque." Leading man to such distinguished actresses as Billie Burke and Ada Rehan, John Drew, uncle of Lionel, John and Ethel Barrymore, was at this time one of the most important stars in the American theater. He was also regarded as the epitome of sartorial perferction.

Reeves himself made a natty figure on the Rialto. He wore a Prince Albert coat and trousers with the stripes attached and a huge yellow diamond stickpin. He was one of the first burlesque stars, if not *the* first, to bring a dress suit with him into vaudeville.

Reeves started his career in variety as a boy tenor at the age of twelve. But he soon graduated to a comedy quartette in burlesque in which he sang and played the banjo. He earned the nickname of "Diamond Al Reeves" because of his jewel-studded banjo, and he claimed the doubtful distinction of being the first man to play a banjo illuminated with an American flag.

168

A good comedian himself, he was quick to recognize ability in others. He was also an excellent businessman and he became one of the greatest of all burlesque producers.

To attract patrons, Reeves advertised a big reception on the stage on Sundays. He sent out also a ten-thousand-dollar challenge that no other show on the road had forty-two girls as pretty as those in his chorus, with an attached parenthesis that read: *Neither Ziegfeld nor anyone else is barred from competing.*

Through his persistence, Reeves managed to break into Broadway. He was a member of the company in which Anna Held made her debut. This captivating French music-hall entertainer implored the gents in the baldheaded row to "come and play wiz me." She was also the heroine of the most famous publicity stunt ever contrived, a milk bath in which she supposedly indulged daily in order to retain and heighten her beauty.

James Barton, the greatest of all drunks and all-round stage genius

Braggart bus driver, garrulous bartender and patrician scapegrace, Reggie Van Jackie Gleason

The list of those who came up through burlesque to hit the heights on Broadway is long: Jimmy Savo, whose burlesque act was a bedroom "bit" and who once lost all his applause to eight preceding bedroom acts on the same bill which had stolen something from his original act; James Barton, whose "mad drunk" scene is unquestionably the greatest in American theatrical history; Bert Lahr, who graduated from one of the funniest low comedians in burlesque to *Waiting for Godot* on Broadway, and whom Brooks Atkinson, writing in *The New York Times,* described as "never more glorious, an actor in the pantomime tradition who has a thousand ways to grimace in order to make the story interesting, theatrical, and touching too!"; gum-chewer Will Rogers of rope and homely wit fame, who rose from cowboy to Ziegfeld star, national sage and author; and Jackie Gleason, who at nineteen served for two weeks as an amateur-night master of ceremonies and subsequently signed the largest contract in the history of amusements — a five-million-dollar television contract.

Among the many notables who had an early skirmish with burleycue were Abbott and Costello; George Jessel, stage star, producer and celebrated M.C.; "Red" Skelton; Rufus Le Maire; Jack Haley; Joey Faye; Rags Ragland; "Red Buttons"; Al Lewis, producer; Jack MacGowan, author of *Excess Baggage* and collaborator on *Girl Crazy* and the screen hit *Broadway Melody of 1936;* William K. Wells, who wrote twelve editions of the *Scandals;* Louis Calhern, star of *The Magnificent Yankee;* and the distinguished producer, once a burlesque advance man, Max Gordon, whose numerous musical and stage hits include *Born Yesterday* and *The Women*, by Claire Booth Luce, Ambassador to Italy. David Warfield, who started his stage life as an usher, played three years in burlesque and then became the brilliant legitimate star of *The Auctioneer* and *The Music Master.*

The few talented women burlesquers had scarcely any chance for advancement. Those who succeeded did so largely on the strength of their physical appeal, large following or power to dominate a show through the ownership or the publicity value of their names. Among the limited number of those who reached Broadway were Fanny Brice and Sophie Tucker.

Amateur nights gave Fanny Brice her first chance to earn her living as a member of the theatrical profession. She sang illustrated songs at a nickelodeon house at Eighty-third Street and Third Avenue, on Thursday and Friday nights.

Ambitious, she finally got a job in a burlesque show and made a hit. They called her a curbstone comedienne but the comedians hated her because she was funny.

Gum-chewing philosopher-comedian Will Rogers

When she finally signed for a fairly good job with the *College Girls* company, she rushed out frantically to the music publishers, Berlin, Waterson and Snyder, for material.

"Hello, Irving," she cried. "I want two songs to sing."

"What kind of songs?" asked Irving.

The question flabbergasted her, to whom songs, at that time, were just songs. "I leave it to you."

Sensing her inability, Irving walked over to the piano and took out two songs, "Cherry Rag" and "Sadie Salome." He sang "Salome" with a Jewish accent.

Abbott and Costello, veteran burlesque comics, risibility experts in kicking a man when he's down

Jack MacGowan, called the best-dressed straight man in burlesque

Up to this time, Fanny had never done a line of dialect. Automatically she followed the composer's lead and sang as he did.

"That was a crucial moment in my life," she declares, "though I didn't know it. If Irving had given me an Irish song and done it with a brogue I would have been an Irish comedienne forever."

The rest is theatrical history. Ziegfeld saw her, signed her up for the Follies, and she wore out eight duplicate contracts folding and unfolding them, showing them to friends.

She became at once one of the most popular comics in America. She imperiled

Grotesque make-up was one of the burlesque media that Fanny Brice employed for creating laughs

her natural comic physical equipment, a crooked nose, by having it bobbed, a pioneer experiment in facial surgery. Her versatility grew with the passing years. She appeared in legitimate drama and on radio. Her "Baby Snooks" was one of the funniest and most engaging characterizations ever to delight the public year after year.

The tenderloin, a forgotten term once the equivalent for another forgotten term, "the red-light district," served as the starting point for the beloved star, Sophie Tucker.

Here, at the age of seven, she was earning her living in the kitchen of a twenty-five-cent restaurant in Hartford, Connecticut, washing and wiping dishes. At fourteen she was a full-fledged "slavey" in a small roominghouse.

Her early performances as a "coon shouter" were the prelude to a popularity that made her a national institution known for many years as "the Mary Garden of Ragtime" and then "the last of the Red-Hot Mamas."

Sometimes she delivered her number standing in front of the footlights with a revolver in hand, pointed directly at the audience.

From honky-tonk she made her way to vaudeville which was climaxed, years after, by appearances at the Palace and the Palladium in London, where she was the pet of both princes and poor folk.

With her increasing success, Sophie's charities increased and her rewards. Her seventieth birthday served as the occasion for a kind of national celebration which voiced the gratitude of thousands for her singing and her humanity. In honor of the occasion she wore a twenty-four carat cloth-of-gold gown festooned with brilliants, a white mink with a golden train, a cloth-of-gold headdress sprinkled with diamonds and bursting forth in sprays of aigrettes.

The climax of this celebration was a banquet tendered by the old theatrical club, the Friars, with Sophie on the dais, the only lady present and happily free to "open up" with a rich repository of stories that were appropriate to the occasion.

Famous burlesque stars of both sexes and burlesque itself were the chief contributors to the creation of that distinctly native entertainment — musical comedy.

Sophie Tucker, last of the Red-Hot Mommas, enjoys discomfort

16

Minsky

When burlesque was banished from the New York scene in 1939, so were the Minskys. As a family, they had been identified with the entertainment world almost ever since Louis Minsky landed in America in 1880. His four sons, Abraham B., Herbert K., Billy and Morton, were born on the East Side. Herbert and Morton basked in the light of degrees from Columbia and New York University respectively; Billy was once society editor on *The World*.

Members of the family were frequently embattled, once, in particular, over the legal rights to the use of the name, which became important in 1920 when the Minskys operated a chain of twelve houses.

Louis Minsky was an alderman and builder. He put up the National Winter

One of Billy Minsky's temples of passion

Garden at Houston Street which, for a time, according to report, served as a synagogue. But the eclipse of two old burlesque houses, the London and Miner's Bowery, led him to believe that there was a growing need for this type of entertainment in the down-at-the-heels Houston district. So he decided to put Billy into show business.

Billy was the imaginative demiurge of the family, who liked to manifest his fancied resemblance to Florenz Ziegfeld, master revue and musical comedy producer of his era.

"Little Ziggy" ran the Garden for a time as a movie house, with specials and super-specials at twenty-cent tops. But business was bad; so Billy turned to burlesque, a medium which gave him the perfect opportunity for displaying his abilities.

The efforts of Sam Scribner and other producers to clean up the entertainment did not perturb him in the least. He threw all restrictions out of the window and from that moment made history in the grand manner.

First of all, taking note of the oncoming change in the female figure, he substituted for the ponderous pets of the past, svelte ladies in their teens and twenties. Next he threw out all the old gaudy scenic and electric effects and substituted in their place simple backgrounds which gave added emphasis to the action and the word; that is, the dirty word.

While thus downgrading burlesque, Billy's ambitions soared, by inverse proportion, to patrician altitudes. He took on a continental swank by advertising his

Celebrated Minsky alumnus Phil Silvers, winner of multiple prizes

entertainment with the euphemistic come-on: *What the Folies Bergere is to Paris, Minsky shows are to New York.* He contrived also to confer distinction by arranging occasional personal appearances of notables like Clara Kimball Young and Mary Pickford. And though the goings-on during performances were sometimes so raucous that guards passed up and down the aisles to maintain discipline, the audience included at times well-bred gentlemen from the Harvard and Racquet clubs, thanks to free tickets which Billy managed to distribute at those select spots.

Sometimes Minsky publicity made reference also to men of distinction before that term became the equivalent for a whiskey bait — men like Horace Liveright, the publisher, Conde Nast, socialite editor of *Vanity Fair*, and Otto Kahn, whose support and guidance of the Metropolitan Association carried it through many precarious seasons.

The slump in burlesque that followed the war and the market crash had a favorable effect on Billy's enterprise. He brought two or three shows right to the heart of Broadway. He went to crime for headliners, employing "Kiki" Roberts, sweetheart of gangster "Legs Diamond."

Triumphal was the opening on Broadway of Minsky's Oriental Theatre, an occasion which celebrated the graduation exercises of stripteasers. The theater was renovated for the occasion. Murals of nude ladies adorned the lobby, and young ladies attired in harem costumes showed the lucky guests to their seats.

The ceremonies were impressive. The not-too-sweet girl graduates wiggled and swerved. Then Gypsy Rose Lee received, *in absentia*, the formal degree of Doctor of Striptease. Gertrude Lawrence accepted the diploma for her and the walls reverberated with applause. The artist Reginald Marsh, inspired interpreter of burlesque, spoke. Aaron Copland, the composer, and Mrs. Busch Greenough, socialite, were among the guests of honor. e. e. cummings was announced to appear but when he didn't show up, someone in the audience called, "You'll find him in the lower case!"

These gala ceremonies had an ignominious aftermath. In order to add a note of distinction to the handsomely engraved invitations, they had been adorned with the emblem of Barnard College.

This desecration of that dignified institution's privacy came to the attention of President Nicholas Murray Butler who, shocked beyond words, became suddenly articulate, called in the police and requested the expulsion of the Minskys from New York theaters.

One of the last Billy Minsky shows presented, for the first time in history,

178

girls doing a "grind" on the floor; that is, while lying on their backs they duplicated all the maneuvers and gyrations of the belly dance, including the "bumps."

However, actors thrive even in untoward surroundings. They are infatuated with their art, an art which in its various forms of expression is perhaps humanity's greatest medium for escape from unhappiness.

Those early actors of the *commedia dell' arte* traveled as far as London, regardless of hardships, to make people laugh and cry. Banned in France by Mme. Pompadour, they returned again to play their parts. In England, a parliamentary ordinance in 1642 deprived the actors of a living. The first women to appear on the stage were slandered. The early Elizabethan actresses were dubbed thieves and vagabonds.

So appearing at Minsky's merely stimulated the ambitions of the early performers who took part in the bawdy shows. Among these was one of the most lovable singers America has ever known, Belle Baker, later the star of Ziegfeld's *Betsy;* Van and Schenck, long-time headliners at the Palace; Cora Green; Hamtree Harrington, whose full talents never reached the audience they merited; and Tom Howard who, with George Shelton and Lulu McConnell, presented the radio hit, "It Pays To Be Ignorant."

In 1934, Phil Silvers joined Minsky's burlesque as humble third banana. For the next five years, half of the time at New York's Gaiety Theatre where he teamed up with the late Rags Ragland, the great "rube" laughmaker, Silvers developed into one of the best clowns in burlesque. In puttied nose, baggy pants and trick shoes he was hit on the head with folded newspapers, spattered with custard pies, drenched with pails of water, pushed over chairs and tables, had his breakaway clothes torn off his body, and was flung sprawling onto the stage floor. Yet he made his way eventually to Broadway as the star of *High Button Shoes.* And for his performance in *Top Banana,* in 1952, he was voted best comedian of the year in the Antoinette Perry, the New York Drama Critics, Billboard Donaldson and Look Magazine awards, and won two TV Emmys.

But even before Phil Silvers joined the Minskys, they were having their troubles.

In 1932, Mayor Fiorello H. LaGuardia outlawed the word burlesque and Minskys. After urgent solicitation, however, and certain political maneuvering, the shows were permitted to reopen providing they substituted the word "Follies" for the taboo burlesque.

But in 1939 the shows were banished for good. Paul Moss, License Commissioner, rejecting the application for a license, charged that "Herbert K. and Morton Minsky cannot be trusted with a license to operate a theater and that doing so would be contrary to good order and public decency and would be dangerous to the morals and welfare of the community."

That the Minskys were largely responsible for the banning of burlesque in

Zorita. Enuff said

MURRAY KORMAN

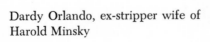

Dardy Orlando, ex-stripper wife of
Harold Minsky

MURRAY KORMAN

New York is a matter of record. For years before the final ax fell, they had been the subject of hot debate in the press. Sime Silverman, publishing genius and champion of the highest theatrical standards, wrote this piece in the February 18, 1931 issue of *Variety,* the "Bible of Show Business":

THE KILLER OF BURLESQUE
MINSKY'S MESS AT REPUBLIC CONTAINS EVERYTHING THAT RUINED BURLESQUE BUSINESS IN U.S. — CHEAPEST DIRT, DIRTIEST COOCHERS AND NO TALENT — JUST ROTTEN

By Sime Silverman

In the new stock burlesque show propelled by the Minskys at the Republic on 42nd Street . . . opening on the day Lincoln was born to free the slaves, are the new slaves to stock burlesque. . . . The new slaves are the chorus girls. Pity them. . . . While in the Minsky mess at the Republic, too inelegant, too dumb and to dirty to be even called a troupe, is everything that has been pushed forward in past years to ruin the name of burlesque. . . .

If any individual in this group is receiving more than $60 weekly, the management is cheated. What the chorus girls may receive is but a guess, but according to a dirty ballyhoo for them, they may be presumed to earn more in the alley than in the theater. . . . A key attached to a card is being distributed around Times Square. It reads: "This key is to the stage door at the Republic Theatre. Our girls don't like to walk."

With two runaways for the 32 girls and for the imbeciles on 42nd Street, the Republic will draw in the curious for a while. They go to see the teasers, weavers and tossers. All there and how — in silhouette, on their feet and on their backs.

Yet the Minskys had their distinguished defenders too. Edmund Wilson, in the *New Republic* of July 8, 1925, wrote:

The National Winter Garden's current version of "Antony and Cleopatra" is particularly gratifying. "I'm dying. I'm dying," groans Antony. Whereupon all the rest of the company — Caesar, Cleopatra, the Roman soldiers and the beautiful Egyptian slave girls — break into a rousing shimmy to the refrain of "He's dying."

"I hear the angels," says Antony. "What do they say?" inquires Caesar. "I don't understand Polack." He is groggy; he staggers; he faints. "I hear the cockroaches calling me," he cries. And from the orchestra is heard the sinister and acrid, the sullen chant of the expectant roaches. When he is dead, Cleopatra applies to her breast what is described as a "vasp." She falls prone over Antony's body, and Caesar places upon her posterior a wreath which he waters with a small watering pot. Then it is the turn of Britannicus and Charmian to die. How this is accomplished the pages of this magazine are not the proper place to record; but when the heartbroken tire-woman falls lifeless upon the body of the faithful follower, she explodes a small toy balloon which she has been wearing as a false chest.

182

Wistful was the tone of George Jean Nathan:

> The Olympic remains true to its first principles and devotes itself to pure un-adulterated and heart-warming old knock 'em down and drag 'em out bur-lesque. Well, here it is from the Gas House Quartette to the Hoochie dames, from the venerable money-changing act to the flossie with the red tie, from the show curtain with the chewing gum advertisement to the boy who sells boxes of candy in the aisles — twenty-five cents, a quarter — and a prize in every box. The good old smell of stale cigars and cigarettes, of cheap hair tonics and Third Ave-nue drugstore perfumery, of the hospitably near, frankly unabashed and doorless "Gents Walk" . . . It is all very gay and just a bit sad. There is a touch of *pense-roso* in its memorable framing of rears, in its cracking of bladders on pates, in its spacious parts and red under-lingerie and crepe whiskers and pink wigs.

Commenting on this impression, Robert Garland said in the *World-Telegram,* June 18, 1931: "Encouraged by the printed enthusiasms of Mr. George Jean Nathan, I sit in the presence of burlesque show after burlesque show. But try as I may, I can never manage to tell one from the other."

One concrete cause for the closing of burlesque is here revealed for the first time by Harry Davies, former press agent for the Minskys.

One day Davies was struck by a newspaper headline: FRENCH ARTISTS ENTER U. S. UNDER GUISE OF STRIPTEASERS.

Hastily he looked for a follow-up on the headline, but finding none, decided that he would visit Washington and appear before the Senate Foreign Investi-gation Committee to enter a formal complaint against the influx of foreign per-formers.

Accompanied by the Minsky brothers, Herbert and Morton, Davies arrived in Washington and, after many ineffectual efforts, reached Senator Dickstein and informed him that he would like an interview that night.

Dickstein refused; whereupon Davies said that he had six stripteaser dancers with him and that if he did not get the interview, they would picket the Sen-ator's office with banners reading: *Senator Dickstein is unfair to the Minsky girl.*

The stripteasers were only figments of Davies' imagination, invented for the occasion to exert pressure on Dickstein. But the Senator succumbed to the threat and agreed to meet the Minskys and Davies in his suite.

When the Senator opened the door to admit these gentlemen, a barrage of cameramen started taking pictures. In a spot, the Senator finally agreed to per-mit the Minskys to make an appearance before the Senate investigation.

As arranged, at nine o'clock the following morning the Minsky brothers took the stand and swore that they never hired a foreigner as a stripteaser and that only American girls represented the standard of the true artist.

This statement made the front pages of almost every newspaper in the country.

The stunt was an excellent one, but it helped kill burlesque.

The last judicial pronouncement on the fate of burlesque in New York City came in April 1942, when Supreme Court Justice Aaron J. Levy declared in a 3,500-word decision that present-day burlesque is "inartistic filth" and denied the application of the operators of a theater closed by the then mayor, Fiorello LaGuardia, for a court order to force the City Administration to renew their license.

Though New York is now deprived of the leg show, Jersey and scattered outposts still display the tattered remnants of what was once real entertainment.

In Newark, Harold Minsky, adopted son of the late Abe Minsky and husband of ex-stripper Dardy Orlando, is apparently living up to tradition by operating a show that faces, according to the papers, almost daily extinction.

Death of burlesque in New York City — Minskys are compelled to ring down the curtain

"Burlesk," by Bertram Goodman — an artist's impression

17

Decline and Fall

During the ten or twenty years preceding Prohibition, burlesque thrived like a stock market boom. The wheels or circuits bristled with industry, clicked off hits, coined money. Then, all of a sudden, the unexpected happened. Business began to fall off, precipitating in an incredibly short time the complete collapse of the entire industry.

The decline and fall were due to external causes beyond control and to internal causes which the producers strove desperately but in vain to control.

The external causes were the loss of the traditional audiences through World War I, the advent of movies and radio, the popularity of the new Broadway revues, clerical and press opposition, conniving politicians and grafting police, Prohibition, the market crash and the Depression.

Internal trouble and internecine warfare, polished off by litigation, changes of management, bankruptcy, arrests, organization of new circuits and stock companies proved too difficult for producers to combat.

A definite financial cause was the sudden power of the stagehands' union and its increasing demands, the same power that killed off a great cultural and lucrative field of entertainment, "the road," the "one-night" stands with famous stars like Richard Mansfield, Maude Adams, DeWolfe Hopper, Mrs. Fiske, Jefferson De Angelos and Frank Daniels.

Nor could burlesque combat the fatal effect of the new amusement medium, motion pictures, with their low admission fees, any more than it could match the hero worship of the silent screen stars like Norma and Constance Talmadge, Douglas Fairbanks and Clara Bow, whose fascinations were heightened by the force of the new fan magazines.

Depression had a dual effect on burlesque. It caused a revival in New York, particularly for the Minskys, and a decline elsewhere. The effect was reflected in the nature of the performances. Up till then burlesque had followed the practice of the legitimate theater by giving matinee and evening performances, but with the Depression the managers tried to cut their losses by adopting "grinds," a new term at the time, borrowed from the movies and meaning continuous shows from early morning to late at night.

Managers made other desperate efforts to keep business alive.

Road companies auctioned off the girls in the show to members in the audience, the highest bidders being given the privilege of meeting the girls after the show for dinner and dates in the company's "privilege" car.

But after the suckers were pleasantly established in their seats with drinks before them, they were interrupted by a fake raid. Terrified, they would rush off the car in one direction while the train went on to the next whistle stop, there to repeat the same racket.

Certain cities tried to institute new policies. Detroit, for instance, ran combination tabloid shows and movie grinds of outworn second- and third-rate pictures for a cut-rate admission price of fifteen cents.

The show itself was a tabloid burleycue with all the old conventions retained: gags, songs, bits, chorus girls and comics. But the entire cast comprised only twelve people: two comics, two women principals and a chorus of eight girls.

Over and over they performed the same show, from five to seven times a day, expressionless faces, tired bodies, mumbled lines, casual gestures — slaves of the stage, mirthless and hopeless. At the end of each show the pictures came on, one after another, blurred and worn. Then about midnight, the picture operator flashed a message on the screen: *Stay all night if you wish.*

Burlesque had turned into a flophouse.

New York producers made desperate efforts to lure visitors. In the Gaiety the doors were left open so that passers-by might get a glimpse. At the Republic, Minsky set up dirty electric signs, using Yiddish equivalents for anatomical parts. And the runway came into being, an innovation which established a brief intimacy between the women of the chorus and the men of the audience. It dated back to the early Japanese No plays, a derivative of the Flower-Way. Legitimate plays like *Sumurun* and *The Miracle* had employed steps leading from the stage into the orchestra for the similar purpose of bringing audience and players into closer contact. But the runway was much more extensive. It reached out into the audience and down the middle aisle and was strong enough to hold the entire chorus. And it put the men who sat on the aisle in an advantageous position for getting a close-up view of the young ladies and for passing up assignation notes, boxes of candy and other cheap gifts.

Another of burlesque's competitors, and wholly unexpected, was an abstract one — Fashion. The minute that the dress designers declared that skirts should be shorter, legs ceased to be a rarity, certainly no longer worth the price of an admission ticket. Make-up was a detractor. Painted women were once called tarts. Now lipstick, rouge and hair dye are associated with conventional dress.

A minor yet undoubted influence operating against burlesque was the use of blasphemy and frank speech in plays like *What Price Glory?* and *Rain*, dialogue which took the edge off burlesque ribaldry. Fannie Brice, simulating modesty in *Sweet and Low,* advised George Jessel when he endeavored to disrobe her to "try the zipper," adding "I'm a voigin."

A continuous menace to burlesque was the opposition of the clergy and the press, which denounced the entertainment as shameful. Other enemies were the conniving politicians and grafting police who used the medium for their own base purposes. At election time politicians made bids for popularity by promising to clean up or eliminate the shows, while the police, usurping censorship, made arrests and dug up violations, promising protection for a little matter of dollars and cents.

But the efforts of certain producers to clean up burlesque had disastrous effects. Hoping to bring back the public, they established their own censors, cut out advertising curtains and blue dialogue, salacious stage business and dirty slapstick. They prohibited smoking in the orchestra, kept the show on the stage, cut out advertising curtains and dispersed the candy butchers. Disgruntled customers, resenting the clean-up, demanded a return of the old smut. Minsky and the stock burlesque came to the rescue.

Oddly enough, one of the strongest destructive influences came from the theatrical world itself, in the form of the revue, introduced by Florenz Ziegfeld in his Ziegfeld Follies and for a time imitated successfully by Earl Carroll, George White and John Murray Anderson. The revue was basically lacquered burlesque. The same bits displayed in burlesque were now labeled "black-outs." Bumps and grinds were presented under the cover of ballet in *An American in*

"Minsky's Chorus" by Reginald Marsh, showing the runway promenade

Florenz Ziegfeld went to burlesque for talent, glorified the American girl, produced the Follies and *Showboat*

Paris, by George Gershwin. Ben Ali Haggin's tableaux in the Ziegfeld Follies showed Lady Godiva riding a horse, and the same revue eclipsed burlesque by featuring famous nudes like Beryl Halley, Faith Bacon and Marian Hurley in the Gardens of Versailles. The success of these revues was immediate. The prices were higher than those of leg shows but they had one great advantage: a fellow could take his girl to see the goings-on with complete propriety.

The fatal force, however, was striptease. It grew to be almost the sole feature of the entertainment. First one stripper came on, and then another and still another. The comics had brief moments and limited attention. The humor was gone. Loud speakers displaced the straight men. The entertainment dwindled to a succession of undressings and the audiences dwindled to what

Lady Godiva rides again in Ben Ali Haggin tableau in Ziegfeld revue

Variety called "epileptics" — sex-starved men whose only physical experience was limited to abnormal concentration on bodies they could see but never know.

Today candy butchers' pictures have no kick. Every newsstand sells pseudo-physical culture and health publications with profuse illustrations of near-nude females and males. Class magazines display advertisements in which women's legs and breasts are a come-on for the sale of toothbrushes, fishing poles, stockings, dresses, hats, beer and practically everything that is buyable.

The taboos on horizontal position, once forbidden in motion picture publicity, are now largely ignored; and the female and male figures, once static illustrations, now come to life on television and in motion pictures, revealing practically every nuance in sexual stimulation, consummated with kisses so long and violent that they embarrass the audience.

The history of burlesque reflects our changing morality and moves. Times and amusements changed. The American revue vanished from the Broadway scene and the term "glorified showgirl" grew obsolete. Soon obsolescent also was Stage-Door Johnnie, once the glittering principal in the "after-the-theater-supper" legend, symbolized by the luxurious words — "a bird and a bottle."

Comedy itself now faces disaster. In the days of burlesque the same joke drew laughs season after season. Audiences enjoyed what is called the joy of recognition, meeting an old friend.

Today that type of enjoyment is outmoded. Radio and television cry "Off with the old," and "In with the new." Everyone, from the five-year-old to the octogenarian, is hep to the wisecrack, knows the tag line. No comic can amuse these days on his own. He requires a small army of writers.

Thus died burlesque — an art whose great stars entertained thousands — stars who in many instances are today the firm foundations of American entertainment.

Change is a constant concomitant of theatrical business, a kind of vicious circle that is indigenous to every form of entertainment expression. Burlesque faded out. Vaudeville faded out. The silent movies gave way to the talkies. The miracle of radio has been relegated to a secondary interest. Black and white television, like black and white movies, is giving way to color. Now everything in motion pictures hangs on the potentialities of the third dimension, a cinematic repetition of Cézanne's fight to depict *plein-air*.

Despite the ill name it bore, burlesque was the poor man's paradise, low-priced, convivial. For an hour or two, at negligible cost, a man could drown his troubles in laughter. The slogan that purged burlesque of its original wickedness and made it the incomparable school of comedy is its best epitaph:

"A merry laugh doeth good as a medicine."

Index

Sullivan, Ed, 80
Sumurun, 188
Sutherland, Ann, 44
Sweet and Low, 188
Swinburne, A. C., 122
Sydell, Rose, 82, 91-93, 106
Tableaux Vivants, 109-17, 189
Talmadge, Norma and
    Constance, 186
Tanguay, Eva, 37, 125, 157
Teal, Ben, 151
Templeton, Fay, 33
Thalia Theatre, 13, 118
Theatre Comique, Minne-
    apolis, 81
Theatre Comique, Washington,
    81
Thomas, Hilda, 44
Thompson, Lydia, 9, 13, 14-22,
    24
Through the Breakers, 84
Thurston's Folly Theatre, 69
Tillie's Nightmare, 46
Tin Pan Alley, 156-57
Tom Thumb, The Great, 11
Top Banana, 137, 180
Toulouse-Lautrec, 41
Trevis, Mme., 20
Trilby, 87
Tucker, Sophie, 171, 174-75
Tumble Down Dick, 11
Twain, Mark, 121,
Twelve-Pound Look, The, 37
Twentieth Century Maids, The,
    87
Twirly-Whirly, 162
Universal Pictures, 91
Up in Mabel's Room, 78
Van, Billy B., 71
Van and Schenck, 181

Variety, 87, 182, 190
Variety Shows, 29
Vaudeville Shows, 29-37
Verdon, Gwen, 137
Vestris, Mme., 118-20
Villiers, George, 11
Vodery, Will H., 151
Volunteer Organist, The, 167
Von Tilzer, Harry, 153
Vultures of Society, The, 46
Waiting for Godot, 170
Warfield, David, 170
Washburn, Charles, 62
Washington Society Club, 46
Watch and Ward Society, 93
Watson, Lew, 46
Watson, "Sliding Billy," 88-91
Watson, William B. (Billy),
    46, 75, 87, 88-91, 147
Watson's Beef Trust, 76, 88, 91,
    104
Watson Sisters, 35, 87
Watters, George Manker, 137
Weathersby, Eliza, 22, 44
Weber, Joe, 68, 161-62; *see also*
    Weber and Fields
Weber, Lisa, 19
Weber and Fields, 46, 77, 80,
    84, 88, 161-62; *see also* Fields,
    Lew
Weber and Fields Music Hall,
    88, 102
Welch, Ben, 106
Welch, Joe, 106
Welitch, Ljuke, 60
Wells, William K., 170
Welsh, Harry, 106
Wesner, Ella, 30
West, Mae, 145

Western Wheel, 82-86, 108
Westminster Theatre, Provi-
    dence, 81
What Price Glory? 187
Wheels, The, 81-86, 186
Whistler, James, 41
White, Frances, 66
White, George, 94, 157, 188
White Faun, The, 13
Whiteman, Paul, 151
Whitman, Walt, 121
Whoop-Dee-Doo, 162
Williams, Gus, 49
Williams, Harry, 98
Williams, Hattie, 157
Williams and Walker Minstrels,
    29
Wilson, Edmund, 182
Wilson, J. S., 151
Winchell, Walter, 153
Wine, Women and Song, 147-49
Winter Garden, 137
Wizard of Oz, The, 167
Women, The, 138, 170
Woodhull, A. H., 82
Woods, A. H., 78
Wood's Theatre, 19
Worrell Sisters, 13
Wrothe, Ed Lee, 106
Wynn, Ed, 33
Yankee Doodle Girls, 106
Young, Clara Kimball, 178
Yule, Joe, 167
Yule, Joe, Jr., 167
Ziegfeld, Florenz, 37, 57, 173,
    177, 188-89
Ziegfeld Follies, 43, 157, 164,
    167, 173, 189
Zittella, Mlle., 49